The View from Asgaard

To Freedom, drawing on paper,
(illustrated in *This Is My Own*,
1940, p. 35).

The View from Asgaard:
Rockwell Kent's Adirondack Legacy

Caroline M. Welsh and Scott R. Ferris

The Adirondack Museum

Exhibit: The View from Asgaard: Rockwell Kent's Adirondack Legacy

Curator: Caroline M. Welsh

Guest Curator: Scott R. Ferris

Publication: Alice Gilborn, editor-in-chief

                     Jane Mackintosh, designer, co-editor

                     Richard J. Linke, Skidmore College, selected digital enhancements

                     Richard and Elizabeth Walker, photography, except where otherwise noted

                     Peg Mauer, indexer

Publication of this book was made possible in part by a grant from Furthermore, the publication program of The J. M. Kaplan Fund.

The paper used in this publication meets the minimum requirements of American National Standard for Information Sciences — Permanence of Paper for Printed Library Materials, ANSI Z39.481984. (∞)™

Library of Congress Catalog Card Number: 99-73330

ISBN 0-910020-46-9

Manufactured in the United States of America

Dedication

For her wise counsel, enthusiastic support, and endless generosity, the Adirondack Museum dedicates this endeavor to our late friend Lynn H. Boillot.

Caroline M. Welsh

For her unyielding support of my work and her perpetual love and kindness, I dedicate this endeavor to my late friend Jacquie Jones.

Scott R. Ferris

Peace on Earth, 1967
Commercial off-set lithograph
Illustrated Christmas letter previously
printed as American Artists Group
cards No. 25462 and FA 29.
Private collection.

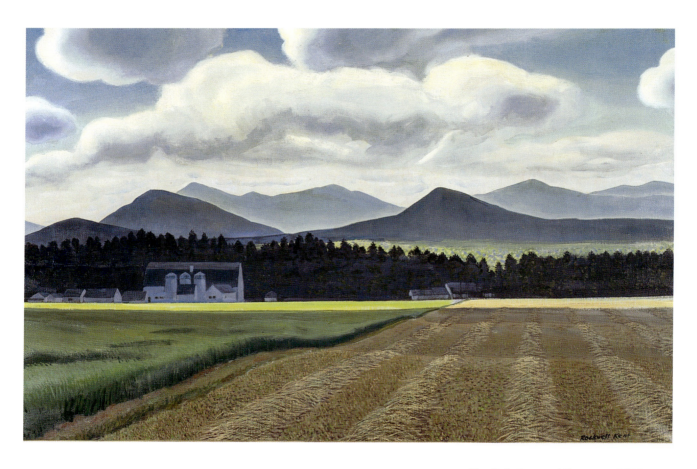

Untitled: Asgaard Farm, ca. 1961
Oil on canvas

The Adirondack Museum, 61.56.1 (44)

Contents

Illustrations viii

Foreword   Jacqueline F. Day, Director of the Adirondack Museum............................ xi

Preface   Shahen Khachaturian, Director of the National Gallery of Armenia
                and Martiros Saryan Museum... xii

Acknowledgments Caroline M. Welsh and Scott R. Ferris xiii

Essay   Rockwell Kent: A Life and Art of His Own
                Caroline M. Welsh...1

Essay   A Greater Luminosity: Rockwell Kent's Paintings and Related Work
                Scott R. Ferris.. 21

Checklist   Selected Checklist of Adirondack Works
                Scott R. Ferris.. 45

References   Selected References, Scott R. Ferris 70

Index   75

Illustrations

All illustrations are oil paintings unless otherwise noted.

Asgaard's Meadows, 1945 . . . . Front Cover

Drawing, *To Freedom* . . . . Frontispiece

Commercial off-set lithograph, *Peace on Earth*, 1967 . . . . [v]

Untitled: Asgaard Farm, ca. 1961 . . . . [vi]

Drawing, *Bringing Home the Christmas Tree*, ca. 1967 xiii

Illustration, *Asgaard Barn*, 1955 xv

Fabric, "Deer Season," ca. 1950s . . . . Back Cover

Figures

1   Lithograph, *Self Portrait*, 1934 . . . . Opposite pg. 1

2   Ceramic, *Our America* Vernonware, ca. 1939 1

3   Fabric, *Harvest Time*, ca. 1950 1

4   "1947 / Asgaard," painted chest, 1947 1

5   Untitled: Asgaard Farm, ca. 1961 2

6   *Au Sable River Rapids*, 1950 3

7   *This Is My Own*, ca. 1940 (study) 3

8   Georgia O'Keeffe, *Storm Clouds, Lake George*, 1923 3

9   *Asgaard in January*, 1958 4

10 Printed socio-political material, 1940s 5

11 Wood engraving, *Mountain Climber*, 1933 6

12 *Scribner's* magazines, 1928, 1929 7

13 Photograph, Kent presenting Christmas Seal art to Franklin D. Roosevelt, 1939 . . . 7

14 Cartoon, "Oh Hell! Rockwell Kent's been here!," 1937 7

15 David Smith, Untitled: Abstract, 1954 8

16 Photograph, Kent exhibition, Moscow, 1957 9

17 Photograph, Au Sable Forks, ca. 1920 10

18   *Asgaard's Meadows*, 1945 10

19   Lithograph, *Roof Tree*, 1928 11

20   *Gladsheim*, 1963 11

21   *Sally*, ca. 1944–49 12

22   Photograph, Kent and children, 1960 12

23   Invitation, Asgaard Farm 12

24   *Christmas Tree*, ca. 1951 13

25   Placemats and menus, ca. 1951 13

26   Illustration, *Public Service*, 1940 13

27   *Winter Sunrise, Whiteface Mountain*, ca. 1952–60 14

28   Silk screen poster, *Asgaard Dairy Milk*, ca. 1935 15

29   Cream and milk bottles, ca. 1934–48 15

30   Logo, Asgaard Dairy, ca. 1934 15

31   Broadside, "Rockwell Kent for Congress," 1948 15

32   Photograph, Kent painting out of doors, ca. 1930 16

33   Photograph, Kent in his studio, ca. 1960 16

34   *Pine Tops and Mountain Peaks*, 1960 17

35   *Mountain Road*, ca. 1960 18

36   *Cloud Shadows*, 1965 19

37   Illustration, *World-Famous Paintings*, 1939 20

38   Illustration, *Life and "Art,"* 1909 22

39   Thomas Cole, *Schroon Lake*, 1846 23

40   *Clover Fields*, 1939–40 24

41   Pamphlet, *The Vigilantes . . .* , 1937 25

42   *Adirondacks*, 1928–30 25

43   *Deer on Palmer Hill*, 1930 25

44   Drawing, *While The Sun Shines*, ca. 1939–40 26

45   *Ancient Elm*, ca. 1961–62 26

46   *Heavy, Heavy Hangs Over Thy Head*, ca. 1946–49 27

47   J. W. Stock, *The Young Hammerer*, n.d. 27

48   Photograph, Kent and *On Earth Peace* mural, 1944 27

49   *This Is My Own*, 1940 28

50   *Skaters*, 1950 29

51   *The Covered Bridge at Jay*, ca. 1950 (study) 29

52   Drawing, *Skaters*, ca. 1950 (study) 29

53   Commerical off-set lithograph, "Buy Christmas Seals," 1939 30

54   *Oncoming Storm: Adirondacks*, 1946 31

55   Drawing, *Oncoming Storm: Adirondacks*, ca. 1946 (study) 31

56   Announcement, Christmas, 1942 31

57   Untitled: View from Palmer Hill, ca. 1950 32

58   Watercolor, "That, for their sake. . . ," ca. 1942–43 33

59   Poster, *Forest Fires Aid the Enemy*, 1943 34

60   Lithograph, *Fire!*, 1948 34

61   *December Eight, 1941*, 1941 35

62   Lithograph, *And Women Must Weep*, 1937 35

63   Lithograph, *Adirondack Cabin*, 1946 36

64   *War*, 1959 37

65   *At Peace*, 1940 38

66   *Hope Springs Eternal*, 1941 38

67   *Wake Up, America!*, 1941 39

68   Drawing, *Life, Liberty and the Pursuit of Happiness*, 1938 39

69   Gouache and watercolor, *Wake Up, America!*, 1941 (study) 39

70   *Russian Mass*, 1928 40

71   *America*, 1939 41

72   *Pastoral*, 1941 41

73   Illustration, *Forest Ranger*, ca. 1943 44

74   Drawing, *Indian Corn*, ca. 1946–50 44

Foreword

The Adirondack Museum is located at the center of the Adirondack Park, a vast mosaic of state and private land that comprises the largest public park in the contiguous United States. Since 1894, nearly half of the Adirondack Park's six million acres have been protected as "forever wild" by the New York State constitution. The changing face of the Adirondacks as a wilderness place is one of the central themes of the Adirondack Museum.

Since the museum opened to the public in 1957, its exhibitions and publications have documented the complex interaction between people and the land as well as cultural attitudes toward nature. The American experience of the wilderness has been in part defined in this region where the reality of everyday life and work was transformed through the myth making imagination of its artists, among them Rockwell Kent.

This exhibition and publication presents for the first time a focused look at Rockwell Kent's Adirondack art and the role that Adirondack imagery played in his creative output. Museum staff and consultants, under the able leadership of Chief Curator Caroline Welsh, have worked with great energy and commitment to bring this important study to the public through "The View from Asgaard: Rockwell Kent's Adirondack Legacy."

Jacqueline F. Day
Director, Adirondack Museum

Preface

Back in 1960, when I was a young employee of the National Art Gallery of Armenia, I enjoyed a unique opportunity to escort Rockwell Kent and his wife, Sally, through our museum. To the great enjoyment of all of us in the Gallery, some days later it received a generous gift of fourteen paintings by the artist. This donation was done by Kent in appreciation of the country of Armenia and its creative people, as well as of our museum, so rich in paintings. "If I were asked where one can see the most miracles on our planet, I would name Armenia." These words by Kent are remembered by many in Armenia.

The works of the American painter were exhibited in Yerevan and elsewhere. One of the visitors left the following entry in the visitors' log:

"I wish I could live in the world of Kent. Peace rules there, people are kind, they seem to work and breathe in God's own lap. God as Nature rules over everything." The perception of Nature as divine has been embedded in the Armenian Christian tradition since early history. Incidentally, it comes as no wonder that a similar kind of perception is characteristic of another renowned American painter, Arshile Gorky, Armenian by origin.

The Armenian people liked Kent's art. Unity between man and Nature is apparently the vehicle of the great humanist's creation. Anchored in the American fine art tradition, the language of Kent, the simple and clear resonance of his palette, is in harmony with the world he depicts and renders it in an epic dimension. The world of Kent is the cold North, alien and amazing. Looking with the inner eye, the artist adds a human touch to reality, appropriates it, and makes it a reflection of his soul. Although his art was born in times of political turmoil and concern, it is permeated with extraordinary pureness and candidness, and these are the virtues that determine its lasting value.

Forty years later, two of the pieces donated by Kent — *Oncoming Storm: Adirondacks*, 1946, and *Asgaard's Meadows*, 1945 — are in the United States at the Adirondack Museum on loan from Armenia. We feel certain that Rockwell Kent's exhibition in his native country shall reaffirm his art's claim to immortality.

Shahen Khachaturian
Director, National Gallery of Armenia
and Martiros Saryan Museum

Shahen Khachaturian is pictured below at the Adirondack Museum in 1999.

Acknowledgments

Bringing Home the Christmas Tree,
ca. 1967. Pen, brush, and ink on
paper. James and Charlene James Duguid.

Museum exhibits have a history. "The View from
Asgaard: Rockwell Kent's Adirondack Legacy" began
with a conversation in the mid-1990s. Rockwell Kent
enthusiast and aficionado Scott R. Ferris had a dream
to take the fruits of his research since 1978 on the
artist and assemble the most comprehensive retrospective of his work ever mounted or published.
Given the Adirondack Museum's mandate to preserve
and interpret the cultural history of its region, we
concentrated on one part of Ferris's dream with Kent's
Adirondack work. Since this body of work had been
little studied and infrequently exhibited, it gave the
museum and the co-curators an opportunity to bring
it to the attention of scholars and the public, in particular, two paintings given by Kent to the peoples
of the Soviet Union which were seen in the United
States for the first time in forty years. For the gracious and enthusiastic loan of these paintings, we are
indebted to Shahen Khachaturian, Director of the
National Gallery of Armenia, who accompanied the
paintings to the United States and who we introduced to Rockwell Kent's Adirondack homeland.

There are many people and institutions to thank
for their assistance with the exhibit. Sally Kent Gorton, the artist's widow, and Linda Dubay, assistant for
The Rockwell Kent Legacies, graciously allowed the
co-curators and other staff to use images for publication, publicity, and reproduction. David and Rhonda
Brunner have been most kind with their hospitality
and cordiality to staff and visitors. The generosity of
the lenders has been paramount; without their cooperation and support there would be no exhibit. Two

neighboring institutions — the Plattsburgh Art Museum and the Norman Rockwell Museum — mounted Rockwell Kent exhibitions in 1999 and 2000: "Commercialism and Idealism: Rockwell Kent — Bringing Art to Advertising" and "Distant Shores: The Odyssey of Rockwell Kent," respectively. Director Edward R. Brohel and Assistant to the Director Marguerite Eisinger of the Plattsburgh Art Museum and Chief Curator Maureen Hart Hennessey and Guest Curator Constance Martin of the Norman Rockwell Museum have shared their knowledge of the artist and worked with this museum to develop collaborative publicity, programming, and a symposium.

The museum thanks Scott Ferris for the exhibit idea and for his unflagging cooperation during the development of the exhibit and this book. His devotion to the artist, his knowledge of the subject, his diligent detective work to uncover minute details and key pieces of information were invaluable to this project. The artist is fortunate to have such a supporter as are we to have this enriched knowledge of long-time Adirondack resident Rockwell Kent. We wish Scott Ferris well in the realization of the rest of his dream.

Staff participated and facilitated the project at all its stages. Director Jackie Day approved the project proposal and enabled its fruition. Tracy Meehan negotiated and organized the considerable logistics for the loans, undertaking international loans for the first time. Jane Mackintosh created the exhibit graphics, posters, and this handsome book with her signature sensitivity, elegant design, and meticulous attention to editorial details. Scott Chartier installed the exhibit with his characteristic talent and cooper-

ation. Karen Joyce performed long hours of word processing and exhibit tasks with patience, forbearance, and humor. Jim Meehan and Doreen Alessi dropped everything to assist with exhibit preparation. Museum editor Alice Gilborn adds another fine accomplishment in this volume to her long list of museum titles. Ann Carroll oversaw the publicity for the project and coordinated collaborative publicity with the Plattsburgh Art Museum and the Norman Rockwell Museum. Victoria Sandiford organized and produced a fine array of reproductions for sale in the museum store. Susan Dineen and her staff schemed and carried out imaginative public and school programs.

The museum is grateful to Furthermore, the publication program of The J. M. Kaplan Fund, for providing partial funding for this book.

Caroline M. Welsh
Chief Curator and Curator of Art

OPPOSITE
Asgaard Barn, drawing on paper,
(illustrated in *It's Me O Lord,* 1955, p. 553).

As Jacquie Jones was to her husband, the late Dan Burne Jones, I, too, have been fortunate to have an in-house aid, editor, and an equalizer in my *koyaanisqatsi*, in one Patricia Gaynor.

Sometimes the best of friendships develop between people with whom direct verbal exchange is limited to a few words that are not native to either, or with people who have never met in person; such have been my relationships with Shahen Khachaturian, and Lana Kazangian, at the Yerevan office of the Armenian General Benevolent Union (A.G.B.U.). I can describe the generosity of and my friendship with Shahen by one act: When I telephoned Shahen to inform him of this exhibition he was first to ask me if I wanted to borrow Kent paintings, and hence the loan of *Oncoming Storm: Adirondacks*, and *Asgaard's Meadows*. It was Lana who subsequently gave verbal and written clarity to the loan agreement that germinated from my initial contact with Shahen. Once again I am in their debt. Anita Anserian, in the New York office of the A.G.B.U., returned to my aid for this latest project; of special note was her introducing us to Arman Grigorian. Arman's fluent English proved most helpful during Shahen's week-long Adirondack visit. Vehanoush Bounarjian; Louise Simone and Sonia Sungarian; Ed, Aris and Janet at *The Armenian Reporter International*, and Assadour Ashdjian, I thank for their advice and assistance.

On the United States side of this effort I am grateful to my co-curator, Caroline Welsh, for her skillful management of the overall project and for her treasure trove of ideas and information, for steering my exhibition proposal through the Adirondack Museum labyrinth, for giving me the freedom to do what I believed to be important, and for beveling the rough edges as we moved forward. We were ably assisted by museum staff throughout the process.

To all of our lenders — some decidedly private — I am deeply indebted. For the unconditional support and swiftness with which they responded to my request, I am especially grateful to Pat Alger, Katherine Blood at the Library of Congress, Florence Cane at Warner Library, Nan and Bill Clarkson, Bob Coleman, Jim and Charlene Duguid, Frederick and Suzanne, Dan A. D. Jones, Leo Spellman at Steinway & Sons, and Deedee Wigmore and Katherine Baumgartner at D. Wigmore Fine Art. For their cooperation and generosity, I thank Sally Gorton, and Rhonda and David Brunner. I also extend my gratitude to Edward Brohel and Marguerite Eisinger, Edward Cantor, Frederick Lewis, Peter Rathbone at Sotheby's, Robin Starr at Skinner's, Sunne Savage, and Eric Widing at Christie's. Never last and never least, I salute my great friends Susan Angell and Tim Palmer, Peter Brady, Kathi and Danny Coane, Gordon Kent and Barbara Kent Carter, David Taylor, and, of course, my mother, for their advice and continued support along the way.

Scott R. Ferris
Guest Curator

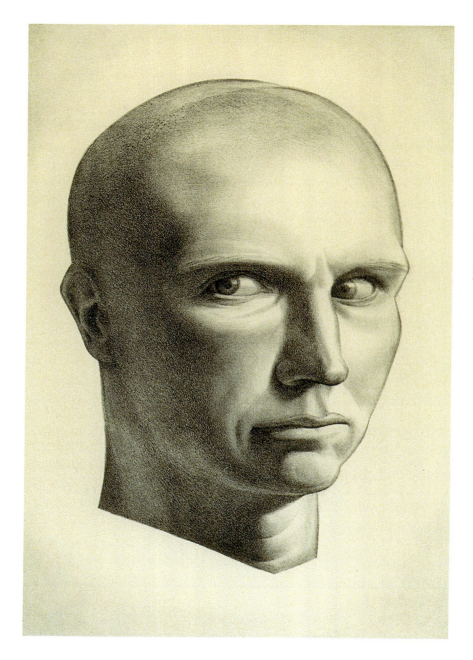

FIG. 1

Self Portrait, 1934
Lithograph on stone
The first variant title,
"Das Ding an Sich,"
comes from an Immanuel
Kant philosophical treatise
and means "The thing in itself."

The Adirondack Museum.
Gift of Pat Alger in memory of
Jacquie and Dan Burne Jones. 99.41.1

Rockwell Kent: A Life and Art of His Own

Caroline M. Welsh

Rockwell Kent was created partly to give the world arresting art, partly to write brilliantly on an adventurous life, but chiefly to demonstrate that nature did not, after Leonardo da Vinci, forget how to make a man who could do everything superbly.

— Lawrence Stallings

Rockwell Kent was more than an artist: he was a Renaissance man in a century of specialists.[1] Born in 1882 and raised in Tarrytown Heights, New York, Kent (fig. 1) studied architecture at Columbia University for just under four years before he left to pursue his first love, painting. Over his life time he created art in almost every medium: canvas, paper, ceramics, fabric, wood, and wall murals (figs. 2–4). He was also a commercial artist, and, in the 1930s and 1940s, America's pre-mier book illustrator. Individualist, adventurer, athlete, Kent was a workaholic who "thought of him-self as a working man whose trade happened to be the expression of a unique view of life through art" (Jones 1975, xi). A fine craftsman, Kent supported his art by manual labor off and on throughout his career. He published and lectured about his travels to remote and wild places. In 1928, he settled in his own "wild place," the Adiron-dacks,[2] where he lived for forty-three years. A socialist since 1904, he espoused many leftist social

FIGS. 2–4

Seventeen-inch theme plate, *Our America* series, Vernon Kilns, ca. 1939. Kent designed more than thirty images for this dinnerware pattern, one of three done for Vernon. The Rockwell Kent Gallery, Plattsburgh Art Museum.

Harvest Time fabric, ca. 1950. Private Collection.

"1947/Asgaard" painted wood chest, 1947. Made by Kent for an employee. One of several constructed and decorated by Kent for household use. The Adirondack Museum. 99.11.1

1

causes. His political activities evoked acclaim and notoriety. This artist, author, activist, and passionate patriot was known as the "stormy petrel of American art" because of his unswerving beliefs about life, art, and the rights of man (Jones 1975, xi). Few other artists provoked such divergent public responses — extravagant commendation to fanatical denunciation — as Kent did over their productive careers (Carl Zigrosser in Jones 1975, x).

Rockwell Kent was first and foremost a painter. All the other mediums in which he worked were primarily means to make a living. James Rosenberg, fellow artist, critic, and Adirondack painter (also Kent's attorney and friend), said in 1920:

> Separate from all the rest of the painters, quite alone, stands Rockwell Kent. Here is a really large vision, a stripping of things to the bone of the essential. The work of a man who is alive and sensitive, as every painter must be, to the methods of others, but who, nonetheless, is simply and only and nothing but Rockwell Kent.[3]

While the native people and icy terrain of Greenland inspired the largest number and best-known of his paintings, his art of the Adirondacks (fig. 5), although less known, is significant because it is an affirmative synthesis of his views on art and nature and life itself. Kent had developed a distinctive style of painting by 1910 after several years' residence on Monhegan Island, Maine. He reduced the details of nature to large, flat, smooth shapes, rhythmic and grand, not abstract but definitely modern. He retained this vigorous yet simple style through all his changes of subject matter and media over his sixty-five year career.

Kent's early aptitude for mechanical drawing may account for his predilection for precise rendering. He never abandoned his early interest in architecture. He worked periodically as an architectural draftsman and designed homes for himself and others. His teacher Kenneth Hayes Miller's strong design and modeling influenced Kent's pictorial organization and figural work. Three of his mentors —William Merritt Chase, Robert Henri, and Abbott Thayer — employed the broad brush strokes and painterly techniques of American Impressionism. If Kent did not assimilate their style, he did assimilate Robert Henri's approach. Henri was a magnetic and influential teacher of a number of Ameri-

can artists at the beginning of the twentieth century. In opposition to the contemporary public's taste for "story-pictures" — complicated, detail-laden, sentimental pictures based on literary subjects — Henri encouraged his students to directly observe life and nature and render these subjects as simple, strong compositions. Nature — more than any art or teacher — guided and influenced Kent (Kettlewell 1974). In this respect, Kent's art is rooted in the nineteenth century, particularly manifested by his preoccupation with the idealized landscape as symbol for the forces

that rule man and nature, and by his joy in the colors and forms of the natural world (fig. 6).

Kent's style shares characteristics with several other artists of his generation, many of whom he knew. Edward Hopper, George Bellows, and Guy Pene du Bois studied at the New York School of Art when he was there. Kent and Hopper, in particular, share an austere social realism and use of raking light (fig. 7). Georgia O'Keeffe (fig. 8), Charles Sheeler, and Grant Wood depicted nature in a hard, smooth, stylized manner like Kent. His friends Jonas Lie

FIG. 9

Asgaard in January, 1958
Oil on canvas

F. B. Horowitz Fine Art, Ltd.

and Marsden Hartley similarly used light and color as message. Strong design elements and themes of isolation and detachment can be seen in the work of all of these artists.

The grandeur of the American landscape has long been the subject of American painting. Early nineteenth-century Americans endowed nature with divine qualities providing man with spiritual and moral instruction. The landscape was a symbol of national identity as well as a metaphor for freedom, abundance, and spiritual renewal (Novak 1980). In the twentieth century, American artists such as Stuart Davis, Arthur Dove,

Marsden Hartley, John Marin, and Georgia O'Keeffe took a new look at the landscape seeking to reinterpret it within the context of modernist aesthetics. In this rubric, nature became synonymous with physical or emotional states; it was a catalyst for personal and intuitive expressions of emotion and mood rather than an external reality to be detailed. In short, modernists painted what they felt not what they saw.[4] In this sense, Rockwell Kent, while realistic in portrayal, is a modernist because he painted what he felt at least as much as what his eyes told him.

The International Exhibition

of Modern Art, known as the Armory Show, opened on February 5, 1913, at New York's 69th Regiment Armory. This seminal event marked a turning point in the development of modern art in America. The exhibit introduced the largest number of European modernist works ever shown in this country together with paintings by American artists in the new mode. The show provoked opposing responses: an increase in abstraction or non-objective painting on the one hand and on the other, a re-entrenchment of traditional, conservative, technique-conscious painting. In the 1930s, regionalism was a manifestation of the latter trend. More than an artistic style, regionalism embodied a set of values that became widespread in the 1920s and 1930s and were popularized further by the economic upheaval and social dislocation of the Great Depression. Regionalism was basically a reaction to the icons of modernization: industrialization, urbanization, and standardization

FIG. 10
Rockwell Kent designed and produced posters, broadsides, calendars, and other graphics to support causes he believed in. Here are a broadside to support his Labor Party candidacy for Congress in 1948; a "Victory" calendar for 1942; and a calendar for the International Workers of the World.

of mass culture. It envisioned the real America as rooted in the natural landscape and in its romanticized past.[5] Aspects of this point of view are embodied in the work of Rockwell Kent (fig. 9).

Rockwell Kent believed that the purpose of art was communication about life. He was one of 3,500 American artists who participated in the New Deal Art programs of the 1930s introduced by Franklin Delano Roosevelt as part of many recovery and work relief initiatives. Between 1933 and 1941, the Public Works of Art Project (1933–35) and the Federal Art Project (1935–41) sponsored the production of some 4,500 murals, 19,000 sculptures, and nearly one million paintings.

Complementing the social realism of regionalism, subjects were primarily historical events, local scenes, and vignettes of daily life depicting an ideal world where man found dignity in productive work, a profound contrast to the harsh realities of the times. Kent envisioned an America which preserved in art all of the nation's cultural diversity (Jones 1975, xvii). This was his link to regionalism. He summarized his credo in his autobiography *This Is My Own:*

> The artists of every generation are merely those who manage to express not primarily their own unique and different thought, but the thought and emotion of the people of their generation or of people everywhere and always. Their interests are expressed in what they do, in what they paint of, write about. . . . The artist is a spokesman for mankind (229).

Kent saw man as the supreme consciousness and art as the "supreme expression of his spirit" (Kent 1955, 224-25).

More than an Artist

Love of art, humanity, and country permeated Kent's work. His concern for the common man and the less fortunate attracted him to socialism. As a young man he was profoundly moved by the late work of Leo Tolstoy condemning the amorality and social injustices of capitalism. Kent declared that at age twenty he was led "to identify myself with the less fortunate of my fellow men, and find in socialism the best — indeed, the only — answer to their needs" (Kent 1955, 469). During his lifetime, he supported left-wing causes and belonged to organizations that promoted world peace, recognition of the Soviet Union, civil rights and liberties, anti-fascism, and organized labor. His support ranged from poster designs to speechmaking to leadership roles in political and service organizations (fig. 10). He helped organize the American Artists Congress and United American Artists and served as an officer for the National Committee for People's Rights and the International Workers' Order, among many others. When the United States government issued lists of subversive organizations, Kent was disappointed that since 1935 he was credited with participating in only eighty-five (Traxel 1980, 178). His radical political stances were reflected in much of his art and nearly all of his actions, and earned him considerable notoriety.

Rockwell Kent drew inspiration from all aspects of his vigorous life. Writing in the introduction to the 1937 exhibition catalogue for the Gallery of Modern Masters in the nation's capitol he noted:

Painting, like words, can serve innumerable ends. It can present a record of man's imagination, it can concern itself with dreams, with symbolizing thought. And it can be. . . merely a faithful record of what my eyes have seen.

His greatest inspiration came from the culture and climes of cold, bleak, polar environments. The stark, austere, elemental landscapes of Greenland, Tierra del Fuego, and Alaska complemented his style. The adventure of it all fed his tempestuous spirit. A wanderer, Kent thrived on exhilaration and danger which served his personal philosophy that art must come from life, and therefore great art required a rich and exciting life. In 1937 he said: "Do you want my life in a nutshell? It's this: that I have only one life, and I'm going to live it as nearly as possible as I want to live it" (Hoagland 1996, 51).

Encouraged by his friend Carl Zigrosser, world-renowned authority on the art of printmaking, Kent himself developed into an outstanding printmaker in the 1920s. He was soon internationally recognized for the dramatic blacks and whites of his engrav-

FIG. 11
Mountain Climber, 1933
Wood engraving printed as an electrotype. After printing, both the electrotype and wood block were sent to Kent for cancellation; he donated them to the Cleveland Museum of Art.
Private Collection.

ings and lithographs (fig. 11). He achieved his greatest acclaim in the 1930s as the most important book illustrator of his time. He illustrated limited editions of the classics; *Moby Dick or the Whale* by Herman Melville was his most famous. He also illustrated his own books like *Wilderness:*

6

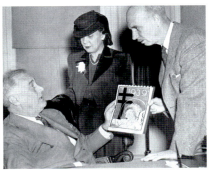

FIGS. 12-14

Kent illustrated several covers of *Scribner's* magazine in 1928 and 1929 with Adirondack imagery.

Private Collection.

Kent presenting Christmas Seal art to President Franklin D. Roosevelt and Mrs. Ernest Grant, director of the District of Columbia Tuberculosis Association, in November 1939.

Courtesy Rockwell Kent Papers, Archives of American Art, Smithsonian Institution.

"Oh Hell! Rockwell Kent's been here!" *Ballyhoo*, January 1937.

Private Collection.

A Journal of Quiet Adventure in Alaska (1920), *This Is My Own* (1940), and *It's Me O Lord* (1955). He was a distinguished graphic designer and typography expert, and, as in his paintings, his style was instantly recognizable (see West 1985). Kent's imagery appeared everywhere: for example, on the covers of *Scribner's* magazines (fig. 12), for the Christmas Seal Campaign against tuberculosis initiated by the National Tuberculosis Association (fig. 13), and for clients like Sherwin-Williams and their 1939 *Home Decorator and Color Guide*. At the height of his career, Rockwell Kent was practically a household word. He was in the news constantly, and his art was in public

buildings, on the walls of museums and galleries, on billboards, on the printed page, and in the popular press. Cartoons in magazines of the day reflect the artist's fame (fig. 14).

Kent's popularity declined in the 1940s partly because modern non-objective art was taking center stage and partly because of antipathy to Kent's vocal support for leftist causes. Kent's opposition to modern abstract art did not endear him to the artistic community nor to the public. He wrote in *Rhythm* magazine (6:1, 36) in 1958:

It is my impression that the most "advanced spokesmen for Modern art" contemptuously repudiate the thought that art should be a means of communication. Quite frankly,

I am not the least bit interested in any form of expression that is not directed to that end.

I am not interested in art but, rather in what art can reveal to me of life.

Ironically, Kent became more famous for his point of view than for his art, as other American artists such as Jackson Pollack, Mark Rothko, and Franz Kline became leaders in the avant-garde art movement. By the 1930s, more than seventy-five percent of America's artists lived in New York City; New York galleries proliferated in the 1940s thanks to a growing interest of collectors and museums in modern American art. Like Kent, the rising young avant-garde artist David Smith — who introduced his abstract sculpture in 1930 — lived and worked on an Adirondack farm (his overlooking Lake George) where he created two and three dimensional abstract art inspired by nature (fig. 15). The American version of Abstract Expressionism, or the New York School, was the most important modernist art movement in the world by the 1940s. This art, in contrast to the social realism of New Deal art, regionalism, and the art of Rockwell Kent, was not about recognizable landscapes or people but was a search for eternal, universal, timeless meanings drawn from the depths of the individual artist's unconscious mind.

From the 1940s into the 1960s, Kent's main subjects were in and around his home in the Adirondacks. He amassed a large body of work that he called "The Great Kent Collection." The domestic political climate in the late 1940s and 1950s was charged with violent anti-Communist feelings, and the period was characterized by suspicion, innuendo, name-calling, and divisiveness. In spite of the fact that the United States had had diplomatic relations with the United Soviet Socialist Republic since 1933, anti-Communist fervor escalated after the end of World War II, and Republicans in Congress declared war on domestic communists as well as foreign ones. Kent stuck to his beliefs, condemning capitalism and supporting his definition of socialism as a constitutional government with equality for all; he overlooked the realities of Stalinism.

When called to appear before Senator Joseph McCarthy and the House Committee on Un-American Activities in 1953, Kent, citing the Fifth Amendment, refused

FIG. 15

Untitled: Abstract, 1954. David Smith (1906–66). Ink and pastel on paper

The Adirondack Museum, Gift of June Noble Larkin. 98.18.1 (544)

to testify or admit to being a Communist which, in fact, he never was. He was profoundly disappointed when he was not permitted to read his prepared speech denouncing McCarthyism as a fascist plot. The rescinding of his passport in the early 1950s provoked him to take legal action all the way to the Supreme Court where Justice William O. Douglas wrote the decision for a five to four vote restoring the right of free travel for United States citizens in 1958.

The price for his uncompromising political beliefs was Kent's career. His work was shunned by American galleries, museums, and the public. In Soviet bloc countries he was acclaimed for his revolutionary ideas and his art. Without an American market for his work, he donated, in 1960, as a gesture of peace, eighty paintings and over seven hundred prints, drawings, and manuscripts to the people of the Soviet Union (Ferris and Pearce 1998). In Kent's words, "art belongs to those who love it most." He made several very well-received trips to the Soviet Union in the late 1950s and early 1960s. There was much publicity about his warm welcomes and the popularity of exhibitions of his artwork there (fig. 16). That, along with Kent's receiving the Lenin Peace Prize in 1967, the prize money from which he donated funds for

medical supplies to aid the South Vietnamese Liberation Front, exacerbated negative views toward Rockwell Kent. Kent defended his political stance:

> People have often asked why I an artist and writer put aside that proper work to engage in political activities. I have answered that if the Adirondack woods are on fire, it is only a question of how close to my studio and home the fire gets before I stop painting and become a fire fighter.[6]

By the late 1960s, Kent's reputation had been restored, and his art was once more in demand. Richard Larcada Gallery in New

York City began selling his work in 1966. In 1969, art historian Richard V. West, Richard Larcada, and the artist mounted a major Kent exhibit at Maine's Bowdoin College Museum of Art. Kent died in 1971 in Plattsburgh just a few months short of his eighty-ninth birthday. The Hyde Collection of Glens Falls, New York, and The Rockwell Kent Legacies of Au Sable Forks[7] (incorporated to preserve, protect, and disseminate the artwork of Rockwell Kent) organized the first posthumous retrospective exhibit in 1974. That same year Kent's third wife and widow, Sally, gave a major gift of oil paintings, prints, drawings, books, and hundreds of ephemeral items including bookplates, stationary, designs, and political advertisements to the State University of New York at Plattsburgh, which created the Rockwell Kent Gallery for the collection. Since the original gift, the Gallery has acquired additional works (among them photographs, fabric, and dinnerware), making it the most comprehensive collection of Kent's work in any one institution.[8] Subsequent sales, exhibitions, and publications combined to further restore the artist's place in history.

FIGS. 17–18

The Village of Au Sable Forks, ca. 1920.

The Adirondack Museum. P49580

Asgaard's Meadows, 1945. Oil on canvas.

National Gallery of Armenia, Yerevan, Republic of Armenia.

Rockwell Kent in the Adirondacks

In September 1927, Rockwell and Frances Kent bought an abandoned 257-acre farm near Au Sable Forks in the Adirondacks (fig. 17). In his words:

> Back in 1927, when I started looking for a farm, I had in my mind such exact specifications that the search to realize them carried us over whole regions of the state and along every highway and byway that survey maps showed. I wanted level land for farming, mountains to look at, and the quiet of a countryside that had not been invaded by summer colonists. One day we came upon the place; the next day we bought it. And three weeks later I had drawn the house plans and let the contract. It was then fall. We moved in the following spring (Kent 1946).

At this time Kent had five children but had divorced their mother, Kathleen, to marry Frances Lee. Together they built a home and renovated the farm and its buildings which he named "Asgaard," Norse for "farm of the gods" (Kent 1940, 141). The house and studio, designed in every detail by Kent, remained his home and base of operations for the rest of his life. Life was busy along the east branch of the Ausable River. Kent orchestrated an elaborate social life with frequent house parties; operated a farm and a dairy business (fig. 18); participated in local and national politics; traveled to wild and lonely places for the adventure and his art; and produced an enormous output of paintings, prints, advertising art, commissions, as well as writing and editorial work.

Kent's plainly defined preconception of a farm extended to the home he and his wife wanted for their "dream house." Kent drew up clear and simple plans for a house which R. Prescott and Sons of nearby Keeseville constructed in four months. Kent credited the workmanship and the speedy completion to the firm's foreman, Moses Rabideau, as well as to the clarity of his own plans. The house, except for the well and the heating system, cost about $13,500 (Hourwich 1929). Frances and Rockwell moved in during the spring of 1928 (figs. 19, 20).

Gracious and old-fashioned,

FIGS. 19-20
Roof Tree, 1928
Lithograph on stone
Library of Congress.

Gladsheim, 1963
Oil on board
Private Collection.

11

Kent's home was set in a grove of pines oriented to face the view of mountains to the west. The living room and bedrooms (eight altogether) faced west, his studio faced north, the kitchen and dining alcove faced east, as did the five bathrooms. Finished in white clapboard and green trim, roofed with weathered shingles, the house nestled into the landscape.

The Kents designed the interior for comfort, hospitality, and to house the art, artifacts, and memorabilia of their lives and travels.

Bright, intense colors on woodwork, unusual wallpapers (Kent used his own navigational maps for his trips to Greenland and around Cape Horn to wallpaper the living room), ingenious built-in furniture and storage spaces, a china cabinet filled with Kent-designed china, and not one inch of wasted space characterized the home. Kent was guided by his belief in the importance of taste. He wrote, "The test of a good

house is how good a time people can have in it" (*Ideas on Decorating* 1941).

The Kents, first Rockwell and Frances and after 1940, Rockwell and Sally (fig. 21), entertained lavishly. Friends from New York journeyed by train (one of the attractions of Au Sable Forks for Kent was easy access to the city by rail for an artist and writer dependent on commissions) to join the Kents, Rockwell's children, and local friends for weekend parties of legendary propor-

FIGS. 21-23
Sally, ca. 1944-49
Oil on board. Kent's third wife, Shirley Johnstone, called Sally, was a frequent model for his work.
The Rockwell Kent Gallery, Plattsburgh Art Museum.

Kent and three of his children: Gordon, Rockwell III, and Kathleen, left to right, 1960.
Photo by Dan Burne Jones, courtesy Scott R. Ferris.

Humorous invitations to Asgaard such as this designed by Kent and signed by his second wife Frances to Bill Kittredge — a typographer with the Lakeside Press in Chicago (the printer for *Moby Dick*) — underscore the lively social life maintained by the Kents.
Private Collection.

tion (figs. 22, 23). Picnics in the surrounding countryside, swims at all hours of day and night in the pool below the house, elegant meals described by his friend, poet and anthologist Louis Untermeyer (Kent 1940, 144), as "gay and gargantuan . . . baronial to the last mouthful," tennis matches, music by voice and instruments, and lively conversation under the sun and stars made for unforgettable times.

The Kents socialized with notables and locals, artists and contractors, farmers and neighbors. Friends and collectors still treasure Christmas cards, valentines, birthday greetings, note cards, and invitations made and sent by the artist (fig. 24). Two artists from nearby Jay, New York, assisted Kent in his Asgaard studio on big projects and sometimes accompanied him to work on site for major murals. For his friend, local restaurant owner Max Lehman, he designed menus, placemats, coasters, and napkins (fig. 25).

As in other settings, Kent was constantly at war with someone or something in the Adirondacks. When the Delaware and Hudson abruptly terminated local service in 1930, Kent lobbied the railroad company to restore passenger service on the branch line, win-

FIG. 24-25
Christmas Tree, ca. 1951
Oil on canvas board. Used as 1951 Christmas Card, American Artists Group No. 15 B 90.
Collection James and Charlene James Duguid.

Placemats and menus for Max's Restaurant and Tirolerland, in Jay, New York, ca. 1951.
Private Collection.

FIG. 26
Public Service, ca. 1940 (detail)
(illustrated in *This Is My Own,* 1940, p. 93).
Private Collection.

13

FIG. 27

Winter Sunrise, Whiteface Mountain,
ca. 1952–60

Oil on canvas mounted on masonite

Collection John Horton.

ning a temporary restoration only to see it rescinded a short two years later (fig. 26) (Kent 1940, 93). In 1933, he took up another losing battle. Many of his neighbors, strapped by the Depression, were in danger of foreclosure on their property because they couldn't pay their taxes. Local inequities in the tax structure favoring the controlling political elite prompted Kent to agitate for reform. His extensive efforts as chairman of the Jay [New York] Taxpayers Association could not displace the local bosses. When New York State proposed to build a road up the side of Whiteface Mountain and a memorial tower at its summit, Kent vigorously opposed the notion verbally and in print. In a letter to the editor of the *New York Times* (April 11, 1934), he argued that a road and tourist trap would violate the very wilderness that Whiteface symbolized and embodied for the viewer:

> Mount Whiteface dominates the Adirondack Mountain region. It stands alone, commanding thousands of square miles. Serene and beautiful, unscarred, unbuilt upon, it is the focal point some part of every day or night for every human eye in view of it. Somehow it does command — not by its height only or by the grandeur of its form, but by that portion of the unchanged wilderness that it holds up for us to see and contemplate; a symbol of immutability (fig. 27).

In spite of Kent's and others' protests, the road was completed and opened by President Franklin Delano Roosevelt and New York Governor Herbert H. Lehman on September 14, 1935.

During World War II, Kent

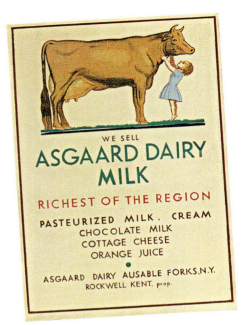

FIG. 28–30

Asgaard Dairy Milk silk screen poster,
ca. 1935. Collection Frederick Lewis.

Asgaard Dairy cream and milk
bottles, ca. 1934–48. The Adirondack
Museum.

Asgaard Dairy logo designed
by the artist, ca. 1934.

expanded his dairy operations to aid the war effort. Along with increasing the size of his Jersey herd, he built his own bottling plant near the barn (figs. 28–30). Production went along well until 1948 when Kent, a socialist since 1904, printed "Vote for Wallace" on the insides of bottle caps and distributed broadsides in an effort to support socialist presidential candidate Henry Wallace, cabinet officer and Vice President for Franklin D. Roosevelt. Long-time customers refused to buy "Red milk," and the resulting boycott prompted Kent to retire from the business. Kent gave the dairy to the two workers who supported him during the boycott, Clifford Malkin and Floyd Plunkett. In his autobiography, *It's Me O Lord* (574), Kent summarized his plight: "Because of a deviation in political belief from the entrenched beliefs of his community, a small business-man — with all in terms of capital and heartache that the rearing of a small, successful enterprise involved — had been wiped out." That same year he ran for Con-gress on the American Labor Party ticket; in the five county election he won less than three percent of the vote (fig. 31). Although Kent's beliefs damaged his reputation,

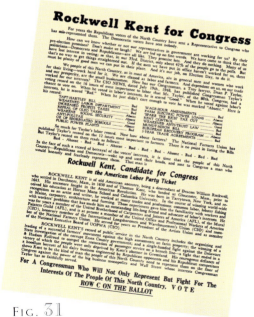

FIG. 31

"Rockwell Kent for Congress"
broadside, 1948. Private Collection.

FIG. 32

Rockwell Kent painting out of doors, ca. 1930.

Courtesy Rockwell Kent Papers, Archives of American Art, Smithsonian Institution.

FIG. 33

Rockwell Kent with *At Peace* in his studio, ca. 1960.

Courtesy Rockwell Kent Papers, Archives of American Art, Smithsonian Institution.

Clinton and Essex county residents on the whole paid little attention to Kent's controversial liberalism (Christiansen 1980).

It was art and nature to which Kent returned from the political fray. The primary focus of his art in his later years was the Adirondacks. In the memoir of his life from 1927 to 1940, *This Is My Own*, he exuberantly recounted his pride and joy in his life and especially in his Adirondack home, Asgaard. Hearkening back to the teachings of Robert Henri in his youth, Kent directly observed nature over and over again, at all times of day, in all the seasons from his own doorstep. From this vantage he saw "westward and heavenward to the high ridge of Whiteface, northward to the northern limits of the mountains, southward to their highest peaks . . . the full half-circle panorama of the Adirondacks." He believed that "it was as though we had never seen the mountains before" (Kent 1940, 48).

Kent worked from nature in several different ways (figs. 32, 33). He made small oil on board studies in nature which he transferred to larger canvases in his Asgaard studio. Sometimes he began full scale compositions on site which he completed later in the studio, and other times he worked from camera or sketchbook studies (Ferris and Pearce 1998, 87). Describing his work, Kent said, "Recording what I could of that deep experience, I would return to Asgaard to refine and clarify those impressions; in other words, to complete the pictures whose essential realities and mood had been established in the Presence" (Kent 1955, 608).

For Kent, the Adirondacks was a different wilderness than Alaska, Greenland, and Tierra del Fuego. Remote from civilization, these places offered the physical and creative challenges Kent craved. He sought the wilderness of Alas-

FIG. 34

Pine Tops and Mountain Peaks, 1960
Oil on canvas

Collection Mrs. and Mrs. William M. E. Clarkson.

remains — smile back at him. . . . It was upon such a wilderness . . . a humanized wilderness that we looked. . . . to. . . farther, higher, steeper, bare-ridged mountain walls to heaven, wave after mountain wave, that wooded, tossing mountain sea of green, the. . . Adirondacks (Kent 1940, 36-38).

ka and later Greenland "for that pursuit of uneventful happiness as the premise for work." Writing for *Arts and Decoration* (June 1919), while in Alaska, he said:

> This sojourn in the wilderness is in no sense an artist's junket in search of picturesque material for brush or pencil, but the flight to freedom of a man who detested the needless petty quarrels and the bitterness of the crowded world — the pilgrimage of a philosopher in quest of happiness and peace of mind. The Wilderness is what man brings to it, no more.

The Adirondack wilderness where Kent lived most of his life was one that he recognized to be, in his words, humanized. Yet, it was still a place where he could be free to pursue his art and life style (fig. 34). Kent wrote:

> And yet for much of the changeless, somber dignity that the Adirondacks have lost [through shortsighted exploitation] we are consoled by the very changefulness which has succeeded it. This much, at least, man in his war on wilderness has done: he has made the wilderness — for wilderness it

Social and political themes receded in Kent's art in his later years as he, like generations of artists before and since, focused more and more on the Adirondack landscape itself. Kent painted what he saw around his home. This was not bleak and lonely like the frigid northern climes but a wilderness rich in beauty of form, color, and light providing enormous variety and endless fascination. When people and animals are present in his landscapes, it is clear that Kent was creating a "peaceable kingdom": man, animal, and nature in harmony. The glowing colors and patterned

17

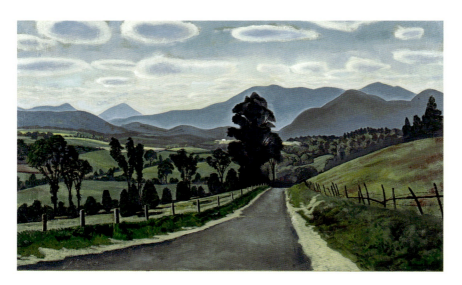

FIG. 35

Mountain Road, ca. 1960

Oil on canvas

The Adirondack Museum. 74.68.1 (356)

shapes of natural forms, light, and shadows gave the artist palpable joy in the paintings he made when he was in his seventies and eighties. He painted the road near his farm, *Mountain Road*, in 1960 (fig. 35). Views of the simple shapes of the farm buildings in the landscape, like the untitled "Asgaard Farm" (1961) (fig. 5), the powerful *Cloud Shadows* (1965) (fig. 36), and *Asgaard in January* (1966) (fig. 9), document the farm in summer and winter. *Clover Fields* (1939–40) (fig. 40) is one of the earliest Asgaard paintings and presages the imagery of the 1960s with its glowing colors and brilliant light. Views of the Ausable River, *Au Sable River Rapids* (1950) (fig. 6), and *Skaters* a.k.a. *The Covered Bridge at Jay* (1950) (fig. 50), hearken back to the documentary style Kent used in the 1920s. *Ancient Elm* (1961–62), (fig. 45) reinforces the solidity, longevity, and strength of nature in this closely drawn magnificent roadside tree. The mountains provided Kent with an unending muse.

In the summer of 1998, I went to Asgaard along the same road the Kents took over seventy years ago. In a metaphysical moment, standing on the knoll above the farm, I saw what Kent saw: the dark green sentinel pines, the "wave after wave" of mountains, Whiteface "serene and beautiful," great sculpted clouds scudding overhead alternately striping the meadows yellow-green and dark (fig. 36). Like a composer Kent played variation upon variation on this theme. His instruments were time of day, seasonal colors — winter white, spring green, summer blue, fall orange — endlessly orchestrated with the changing effects of color and light on the land. Awesome yet serene, timeless yet ever-changing, majestic yet intimate — the Adirondack wilderness still remains the mes-

Fig. 36
Cloud Shadows, 1965
Oil on canvas

Robert Coleman Family Collection.

sage, inspiration, and stimulus for the creative urge. Rockwell Kent's paintings are a singular contribution to the art of the Adirondacks and an affirmative coda to his often tempestuous life as "the stormy petrel of American art."

Notes

1. Dust jacket text by Lawrence Stallings (author, critic, and playwright) on trade edition of *N by E* (Kent 1930).

2. "The all but highest, all but wildest, nearest, most accessible to us: the Adirondacks" (Kent 1940, 18).

3. "Our friend, our counselor (in all but politics), our prop in matters of common sense, and our attorney in that business of uncommon senselessness, the law: James Rosenberg" (Kent 1940, 29).

4. Barbara Haskell and Ruth Stevens Appelhof (1988). In *The Expressionist Landscape: North American Modernist Printing*, 1920–1947. Birmingham, Alabama: Birmingham Museum of Art.

5. Donna M. Cassidy (1994). "On the Subject of Nativeness . . . ," in *Winterthur Portfolio* 29 (Winter).

6. Rockwell Kent to an unidentified American author, 1961, as quoted in Miriam Soffer (1985). "Where He Drew The Line." NAHO 18 (Summer): 14.

7. The name of the village is currently spelled Au Sable Forks or Ausable Forks on maps and in directories and sometimes AuSable. The name of the river (and valley) is spelled Ausable. Kent used two spellings — Au Sable and Ausable — but not AuSable.

8. The Kent Collection at Columbia University's Rare Book Manuscript Library and the Archives of American Art house the majority of Kent's letters and papers. Columbia's collection of Kent drawings is comprehensive. SUNY Plattsburgh's collection of paintings, drawings, prints, advertising art, ceramics, and publications (books, magazines, newspapers) is the most comprehensive of all repositories. Other rich collections are at Princeton University and the Philadelphia Museum of Art.

When the maxims
come to read Art, science,
religion, labour all for
Life's sake, only then
can that perfection of life
which we long for and
which nature works for
be achieved.

— Rockwell Kent,
Daybook, circa 1906

FIG. 37
Title page illustration,
World-Famous Paintings, 1939.

A Greater Luminosity: Rockwell Kent's Paintings and Related Work

Scott R. Ferris

It was almost evening,

the fields that lay before

us were richly lit, as if the

sun that had poured itself

into the earth all day, all

season long, were now

being released through

bark and foliage.

— Jane Urquhart,

The Underpainter, 1997

From Rockwell Kent's earliest writings we experience his heart-felt longing for a sense of place in the physical world, as well as a desire to attain spiritual resolve. Although much has been said about the technical instruction Kent obtained while attending Columbia University's School of Architecture, and that which he received from his mentors William M. Chase, Robert Henri, Abbott Thayer, and Kenneth Hayes Miller, little has been written about his conceptual foundations. Despite his thorough training, Kent was inspired most by life itself. "The greatest feelings of life are universal," he wrote, and it was nature — his life-long mentor — that served as his "ever present conditioner," as well as the pri-mary motif through which he conveyed his thoughts (Kent 1906; 1955, 526).

The signposts in life that Kent followed included rigorous labor, literature, and music. As a young man on Monhegan Island, Maine, he dug wells and privies, harvest-ed lobsters, and built homes, and in his later years he operated a dairy farm. Kent's use of literature in his quest for self-awareness began in the library of his child-hood home and expanded with the encouragement of Henri and Thayer. He was exposed to and found inspiration in the writings of Emerson, Thoreau, Whitman, the Bible, and Darwin's *On the Origin of Species*; he experienced, with lesser effect, Ernst Haekel, Henri Amiel, and Schopenhauer. He loved the Romantic poets, Wordsworth, Coleridge, Byron, Keats, and Shelley; he enjoyed William Blake, Richard Wagner's prose, Goethe's *Wilhelm Meister*, and Shakespeare. Kent specifically attributes to Abbott Thayer his introduction to Kropotkin's *Mutual Aid a Factor of Evolution*, and the Norse Sagas, the latter of which opened the gateways to his northern travels. In music it was the opera (*Lohengrin, Tristan*), American traditional and spiritual, and the German *lieder* of Robert Franz. Kent believed J. S. Bach to be "a glorious draughtsman [whose] lines of melody and his manses of tone are marvelous. A great tonal architect!" Whereas such contemporary composers as Stravinsky and Gershwin had talked about returning to Bach, Kent also believed that the visual artists were going back to "the primitives," referring to "the old masters who came not so long before Bach. Back to men who painted life as they felt it through their eyes" (*Dean of Painters...*1934).

One of the most influential, early guideposts that Kent came upon was Leo Tolstoy's essay, "What is Art?" "And suddenly," Kent recalled in his 1955 autobiography *It's Me O Lord*, "it was as though my whole being had achieved the power of utterance, as though a God within me spoke, resolving the chaos that was me—my mind, my heart, my conscience—into an integrated man, aware and purposeful." Especially noteworthy is this passage that Kent highlighted in his copy of Tolstoy's work (fig. 38).

The destiny of art in our times consists in this: To translate from the region of reason to the region of feeling the truth that the well-being of people

consists in their union, and to substitute for the present kingdom of force, the kingdom of heaven, that is, love, which presents itself to us all as the highest aim of human life (Kent 1955, 91).

Kent's response to Tolstoy's "impassioned exhortation" was an ingenuous, "Amen" (Kent 1955, 92). For Kent, the integration of art and social conscience was the key to unlocking the door to his path in life.

A Discernible Emersonian Voice

"From within or from behind, a light shines through us upon things and makes us aware that we are nothing, but the light is all. A man is the facade of a temple wherein all wisdom and all good abide," wrote the American transcendentalist Ralph Waldo Emerson.[1] Kent parallels Emerson in much of his thought and writing. Of mutual concern to these men was the sentiment that "art has not come to its maturity if it does not put itself abreast with the most potent influences of the world."[2] As with Tolstoy, these influences included peace and brotherhood, the plight of the laboring masses, and "the literal acceptance of the moral teachings of Jesus" (Kent 1955, 92).

Kent was coming into his own when the world-wide rift between the social classes was noticeably growing. Having been raised in the precarious situation of genteel poverty, he became sympathetic to the truly less fortunate. His understanding of Christian ethics was translated, politically, into socialism, and his adherence to fundamental socialist philosophy remained with him the rest his life. In 1904 he signed on to the Socialist party platform — child labor laws, an eight hour work day, labor's right to organize — and in 1948, when he ran for a congressional seat under the American Labor Party banner, his own platform espoused: "Peace and abundance . . . labor's right to full employment and good pay. . . security for small business . . . the preservation of our liberties," and prosperity in a "contented nation in a world at peace."[3]

Robert Henri once observed that "the very things [Kent] portrays on his canvas are the things he sees written in the great organization of life; and his painting is a proclamation of the rights of man, of the dignity of man, of the dignity of creation. It is his belief in God. It is what art should mean"

FIG. 39

Schroon Lake, 1846
Thomas Cole
(1801–48)
Oil on canvas

The Adirondack Museum.
65.3.2 (101)

(Kent 1955, 198). Kent believed that "in that act of re-creation, which is art," he was copying God (Kent 1955, 138).

However, Kent's was not a literal translation but rather a portrayal of the essence of his subject: "The greatest, most powerful, thoughts that nature arouses in us are not of herself but of human life[,] and art should be a record of these thoughts not merely of the physical beauty of the scene" (Kent 1906). Again, the similarities between Kent's thoughts and those of the transcendentalists are striking. Emerson dwelled a little deeper on this topic when he wrote, "the best of beauty is a finer charm than skill in surfaces, in outlines, or rules of art can ever teach, namely a radiation from the work of art, of human character."[4] Thomas Cole (fig. 39) took this thought a step further by suggesting that "if the imagination is shackled and nothing is described but what we see, seldom will anything truly great be produced" (Clark 1975).

Several of Kent's later Adirondack canvases exemplify this reductive approach, including *Asgaard's Meadows* (fig. 18), *Pine Tops and Mountain Peaks* (fig. 34), *Cloud Shadows* (fig. 36), *Ancient*

F I G. 40

Clover Fields, 1939–40

Oil on canvas

Mead Art Museum, Amherst College,
Gift of Mrs. Robert A. Arms in memory
of Robert A. Arms (Class of 1927).

Elm (fig. 45), *Mountain Road* (fig. 35), and *Asgaard in January* (fig. 9). By reducing trees, fields, mountains, and clouds to modeled forms, and layering these forms in distinct, overlapping planes that recede to the horizon, Kent transposed luminism into twentieth-century prose.[5]

Clover Fields (fig. 40) and *Winter Sunrise, Whiteface Mountain* (fig. 27) take a humbler approach to conveying Kent's spirituality by drawing our attention to a narrow band — or patch — of light in the distance. A sense of reverence is inferred as he entices the viewer through shadowy foreground detail toward this band that is compressed by the muted sky above. It is as if the luminosity derives from the candles of a secret ceremony. For Kent, finding truth in light was both a technical and spiritual quest.

"Light was the first of painters,"[6] Emerson wrote; "a jet of pure light" was "the reappearance of the original soul."[7] Kent, like the luminists, took this interpretation to heart and re-created the same philosophy on canvas.

The Figure as Allegory

Walt Whitman in *Leaves of Grass* wrote, "(Ah little recks the laborer, / How near his work is holding him to God, / The loving Laborer through space and time.)" Like Whitman, Kent's imagery flows with a playful rhythm that is laden with romantic nationalism. He believed that "a truly native American art [included] all the characteristics of subject (the American scene) and of method (realism) that are not only proper but absolutely essential to the art of a Democracy" (Kent 1955, 519-520).

For Kent, the graphic arts — book illustration, and especially wood engravings and lithographs (which he considered multiple originals) — were the most democratic of the arts. In each of these three categories he excelled and therefore successfully broadened the audience for his message. To the uninformed, Kent's use of the brush, pen and ink was frequently mistaken for his wood engravings. As an architectural student Kent was taught how the brush could supplant the pen as a means to convey both fine line and the broad, seamless wash. With ink and crayon he created illustrations

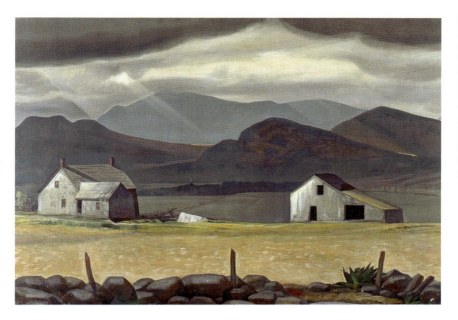

FIGS. 42 - 43

Adirondacks, 1928–30
Oil on canvas

In the Collection of the Corcoran Gallery of Art, Museum Purchase, William A. Clark Fund.

Deer on Palmer Hill, 1930
Oil on canvas

Private Collection.

FIG. 41 *The Vigilantes Hide Behind The Flag,* 1937. Pamphlet published by International Labor Defense. Private Collection.

for *Moby Dick* (1930), *The Complete Works of William Shakespeare,* and *Leaves of Grass* (both 1936), his own books *This Is My Own* (1940) and *It's Me O Lord* (1955), and the posters *Forest Fires Aid the Enemy* (1943) and *Student Christian Association Movement* (1947), among others. Through a variety of printing techniques — line cut and electrotype included — the artist was able to mass produce his realistic imagery in an even greater diversity of formats (fig. 41).

Several of Kent's later paintings use figures or symbols of mankind's presence as devices to identify our place in the physical world. In his earliest of Ausable valley landscapes — *Adirondacks* and *Deer on Palmer Hill* (figs. 42, 43) — dilapidated structures and stumps of harvested trees are symbolic of mankind's temporal existence. *Adirondacks,* in particular, portrays "the tragedy inherent to a region once populous and prosperous" (Kent 1955, 437). This statement by Kent is somewhat misleading. Cultivable land around the High Peaks region of the Adirondack Park (depicted

Figs. 44–45

While The Sun Shines,
ca. 1939–40
Pen, brush, and ink
and crayon on paper

The Adirondack Museum.
Gift of Pat Alger in memory of
Jacquie and Dan Burne Jones. 99.41.2

Ancient Elm, ca. 1961–62
Oil on canvas

Private Collection.

here) was and is scarce, due to the nature of the terrain. Kent did belong, however, to a greater association of North Country farmers (fig. 44) — covering much of the northern tier to the Canadian border — who farmed lands that were more accessible than those in his immediate area. It is also quite true that portions of the Adirondacks were heavily harvested for various minerals and still are today for timber. During these periods of heightened activity, workers often came in droves, establishing temporary communities that simulated prosperity (the

ghost town at Tahawus is witness to this). Some people settled in the region; others fled in search of new employment. Therefore, *Adirondacks* may be interpreted as a symbol of the times in which it was created (the beginning of the Great Depression), the often harsh conditions of life in the Adirondacks, or in a more literal sense, a record of the landscape near Asgaard Farm before Kent made it his home (he removed dilapidated farm structures to make way for his own buildings).[8]

The painting *Ancient Elm* (fig. 45) — lush in high-summer green-

HEAVY, HEAVY HANGS OVER THY HEAD

FIG. 46–47
Heavy, Heavy Hangs Over Thy Head, ca. 1946–49.
Oil on canvas

Courtesy The Baltimore Museum of Art: Purchase with exchange funds from Edward Joseph Gallagher III Memorial Collection. BMA 1991.11

The Young Hammerer
J. W. Stock (n.d.)
Oil on canvas

Courtesy New York State Historical Association, Cooperstown, N. Y.

FIG. 48
Kent with mural, *On Earth Peace*, 1944, located in the Hearing Room, Committee on Merchant Marine and Fisheries, Longworth House, Washington, D. C. Landscape includes a depiction of Asgaard Farm at left edge, below Kent's right hand.

Courtesy Rockwell Kent Papers, Archives of American Art, Smithsonian Institution.

ery — is rendered with fluid brush strokes in modeled forms that resemble the oils of Charles Burchfield and Fairfield Porter. Kent's bold, centralized portrait of this majestic elm invites a somewhat unconventional comparison between this painting and his child-portraits, *My Daughter Clara*, and *Heavy, Heavy Hangs Over Thy Head* (fig. 46). In all of these portraits the main subject is virtually thrown into the arms of the viewer, making no mistake as to what or whom is portrayed. These child-portraits, in particular, are similar to folk portraiture (fig. 47) in another way; they both provide information about the "sitter" in the composition around them. In the painting *Heavy, Heavy Hangs*, the backdrop scenery is Kent's idealized Adirondacks, and in *My Daughter Clara*, his romanticized Newfoundland. Kent employs a similar autobiographical method in his murals *On Earth Peace* and *Mail Service in the Tropic and Arctic Territories*. In the lower left corner of *On Earth Peace*, he incorporates an aerial view of his farm Asgaard (fig. 48), and in *Mail Service*, he places himself in the cockpit of the plane about to depart from Alaska.

The paintings *This Is My Own* (fig. 49), *Asgaard's Meadows* (fig. 18), and *Clover Fields* (fig. 40),

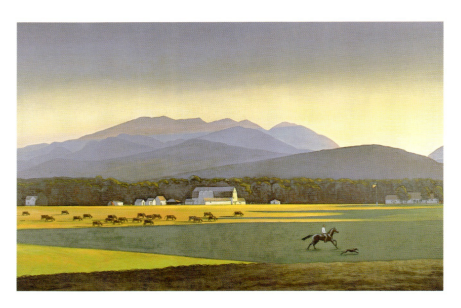

portray the romantic or sentimental side of Kent. They are
in essence the backdrop in *Heavy,
Heavy Hangs Over Thy Head*,
the story of Rockwell Kent in
the Adirondacks. Compositionally
they share Kent's hallmark horizontality in which stacked, com-
partmentalized planes move the
viewer's eyes up through the
canvas. Kent "secures his pictorial
balance . . . by his massive treatment of nature . . . and then by
the power with which he defines
a long flowing contour," wrote
Royal Cortissoz in his review of
Kent's landmark traveling exhibition "Know and Defend America"
(1942–43).[9] The horizontality

that the artist creates is more
obvious in the study for *This
Is My Own* (fig. 7), which does
not possess any of the figural
elements. Contrasting shadows
and sunlight, confined architectural structures, and overlapping
individual mountains are (quite
literally) modeled forms stretching
the dimensions of the board.

Kent is often criticized for
adding figures to completed paintings; this is especially true with his
later work. This practice was usual-
ly misinterpreted as being the act
of an aged, disoriented artist, when
in fact his intentions were deliber-
ate. In the process of creating
Skaters (fig. 50), Kent produced a
small oil study (fig. 51) of the basic
landscape elements and pencil
sketches of the figures (fig. 52).
The artist likewise produced pencil
sketches for the numerous figures
depicted in *Asgaard in January*,
originally titled *Home from School,
Asgaard* (fig. 9). In both of these
paintings Kent worked up his
studies on the larger canvases in
his studio. It is believed that he
executed his painting *Au Sable
River Rapids* (fig. 6) in the same
manner. To support this hypothe-
sis, one can examine the development of the related composition

Au Sable Rapids: Adirondacks.
Numerous pencil sketches have
been found for this work, and a
smaller, similar view of the Ausable, entitled *Spring Freshet* pre-
cedes it.

In Kent's early work his figures
are very painterly and blend in
with the overall composition. Perhaps as a result of the artist's regu-
lar attendance of dance perform-
ances — including those by Isadora Duncan and the Follies — these
figures often take on the appear-
ance of "wispful" dancers. In his
later work, however, Kent's figures
are considerably more rigid and
angular, almost decorative; they
often contrast with the more elo-

quent landscape. Consequently,
they tend to visually rise to the
surface of the canvas in much the
same way as folk portraiture.
Their mannequin-like positioning
resembles the figures the artist
created for Westinghouse (1931)
or the 1939 Christmas Seal (fig.
53), and like them, they successfully convey a story line.

Aside from the obvious message (*Skaters* and *Asgaard in January* are aptly titled for the activities depicted), Kent's figures also
provide insight into how an artist
perceives society, and, perhaps,
how this artist perceived children
(his own were raised in the Victorian manner of prescribed dis-

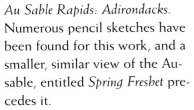

FIGS. 50-52
Skaters, 1950
Oil on canvas
Private Collection.

The Covered Bridge at Jay,
ca. 1950 (study)
Oil on canvas board
Private Collection.

Skaters, ca. 1950 (study)
Pencil on paper
The Adirondack Museum. 99.10.2

tance). In this respect Kent's figures anticipate the sculptural work of George Segal and Duane Hanson in that they become a reflection of how we envisioned ourselves at the moment of compositional creation. For Kent, we as humans divorced ourselves from our natural origins, became materialistically dependent, and in the process, lost our spirituality. His mannequin-like beings, not unlike those produced by contemporary fine and performance artists, addressed this spiritual void just as we currently address the new conundrum, virtual reality.[10] Perhaps Kent again had Emerson in mind when he created these "artificial life forms." Although Emerson might have argued that "artificial life" is also "natural,"[11] he did state that "the beauty of nature must always seem unreal and mocking, until the landscape has human figures, that are as good as itself."[12]

In the compositions *Oncoming Storm: Adirondacks* (fig. 54),*December Eight, 1941* (fig. 61), *At Peace* (fig. 65), and *Wake Up, America!* (fig. 67), the figure or figures are more allegorical. Like the children in *Skaters* and *Asgaard in January,* the bare-breasted, bucket-toting

male in *Oncoming Storm: Adirondacks* is a defining element in the story-telling title, but in contrast to the former paintings, he was somewhat meaningless in the context of its original title, *The Au Sable Valley.*

The meaning behind *Oncoming Storm: Adirondacks* (fig. 54; study is fig. 55) is apparent only after the date of the painting's execution is taken into consideration. In 1946 the oncoming storm, symbolized by the ominous cloud, was the fledgling Cold War. Former allies, the United States and the Soviet Union in particular, were then in the throes of combating ideologies. This convinced Kent "that only tolerance of each other's way of life by the two great powers would ensure lasting, world-wide peace" (S. Kent 1971). He wrote to Pavel P. Mikhailov, Acting Consul General of the U.S.S.R., "In these days, when the promotion of international distrust appears to be the main business of many people and interests, I feel it almost as a spiritual need to drop in at the Consulate and embrace you all" (Kent to Mikhailov, 11 Oct. 1945). The Kents had extended their hands in peace repeatedly. On one other occasion they invit-

FIG. 54-55

Oncoming Storm: Adirondacks, 1946
Oil on canvas
National Gallery of Armenia, Yerevan, Armenia.

Oncoming Storm: Adirondacks,
ca. 1946 (study)
Pencil on paper
The Adirondack Museum. 99.10.4

ed fifteen Soviet students (fig. 56) from Columbia University to share in their Christmas (1942) celebration; twelve attended.[13]

In *Oncoming Storm: Adirondacks,* Kent reverses the natural order of things to depict the ominous cloud bank — a metaphor for the Cold War — as approaching from the east. This suggests that the Great War in the European theater was largely responsible for the Cold War. The position of the young man — apparently a farm laborer — facing away from the oncoming storm, suggests that he is either oblivious to the storm or that he is well aware of the oncoming peril and is moving west — to the home front — to douse the growing conflagration. Preliminary pencil sketches and related works lend credence to the latter interpretation. In one pencil sketch the artist considers the layout of the composition by placing a female figure, carrying a bucket

GREETING

MR. *and* MRS. ROCKWELL KENT
*have the honor to announce that the fifteen students
from the Soviet Union
now attending Columbia University:*

NINA EFREMOFF   JINAIDA GRACHEVA
TAISIA IGOTOVA   VERA ELKINA
IRINA KURITZINA   NINA REPINA
OLIMPIADA SOKOLOVA OLIMPIADA TRONOV
GALINA TZIGANCOVA   MIKHAIL CHERKASOV
SEMEN GONIONSKY   PAVEL SHOKHOV
NIKOLAY SIMENKOV   ALEXEI SOKIZKIN
MIKHAIL IRAEVSKY

will be AT HOME *throughout the Christmas Holidays*
at ASGAARD, AUSABLE FORKS, N. Y.

FIG. 56

Christmas greeting, 1942, announcing that fifteen Soviet students would visit the Kents at Asgaard Farm over the holiday season.

in one hand and pulling a child in another, racing ahead of a male who is laden with buckets in both hands. A second sketch (fig. 55) takes the concept of three fleeing figures one step further by studying the individuals in greater detail. A third sketch, depicting the bucket-toting male standing alone and facing the opposite direction — so as to observe the storm — supports the suggestion that he is en route to douse the conflagration. Kent, as we know by the finished canvas, did not proceed with the use of three figures to convey his message. Instead he reverted to the solitary male figure — erect, arms taut, marching forward — thus main-

taining an air of ambiguity. However, by Kent's re-titling the painting and an examination of some related works, the artist's intentions are made clear.

Kent exhibited this painting as *The Au Sable Valley* in both the Carnegie Institute's "Painting in the United States" (1948), and in the "25th Annual National Art Exhibition" (1949) held at Springville (Utah) High School Art Gallery. Between these exhibitions and the 1957–1958 Soviet tour of Kent's work, the artist changed the title to *Oncoming Storm: Adirondacks*. By making this change — without altering the composition — Kent suggests that we refocus our attention away from the panoramic valley view and toward the male figure shrouded by ominous clouds. Two related paintings — *Green Valley* and Untitled: View From Palmer Hill (fig. 57) — offer figureless landscapes from this same location without straying into a deeper meaning. In an earlier study for a pro-democracy poster (Columbia University), Kent utilized the now familiar erect male figure — a boy — marching forward, but he heightens the effect of his statement by including the "sentimen-

tal, old-time" elements of a Norman Rockwell composition (Kent 1936). An adoring girl races along beside the determined boy; the boy is adorned in the knickers of a by-gone school dress code and is carrying a long, rifle-like branch. They are both parading before a distant little red, one-room school house with an over-sized flag unfurled by the breeze; the backdrop to this scene is an Adirondack-like mountain range. Clearly the physical stance of the male figure in this study represents something more than just a boy on an afternoon walk, and, in fact, it is an important element of the pro-democracy statement. The same can be said of the posturing bare-breasted male in *Oncoming Storm: Adirondacks*, whom we now understand to represent an active player in promoting peace in a world being torn apart by the oncoming Cold War. This posturing element appears in numerous propaganda compositions, including Aleksandr Samolhvalov's 1924 poster *Long live the Komsomol* [Communist Youth League].[14] If there was any doubt as to the purpose of Kent's poster study, he reinforces it by including the caption, "That, for their sake, government of the people, by the people, for the people, shall not perish from the earth" (fig. 58).

Kent was the ultimate recycler. He would often use stationery and scraps of studio paper rather than sketch pads to render his concepts, and as a designer he would often reuse one compositional element to develop another idea. The above mentioned preliminary sketches of a woman and child racing — for *Oncoming Storm: Adirondacks* — appear again in a study for another wartime poster, but this time the woman is clutching children in both arms. This study shows the figures running from a forest fire that has consumed their home, while men battle the blaze. In two similar and conceptually progressive studies, the female figures are eliminated in favor of a solitary male, and the caption "Forest Fires Are Axis Fires,

Volunteer to Fight Them!" evolved to become, *Forest Fires Aid The Enemy, Volunteer to Fight Them* (fig. 59).[15] Several of Kent's poster proposals never came to fruition despite his petitions to President Roosevelt, William Phillips of the Division of Information at the Office for Emergency Management, and others, but *Forest Fires Aid The Enemy* did. It was produced in November of 1943 by the Office of Civilian Defense (Kent 1955, 543-546; Stanley 1989).

The solitary male figure, standing before a backdrop of flames and bracing a double bladed ax, lifts his left hand to his mouth to command the reader to "Join the forest fire fighters service." A more refined variant on this same theme was printed as a lithograph, without text, five years later. *Fire!,* as this composition is titled, shows the fire fighter facing the opposite direction (fig. 60). This suggests that Kent traced over either the poster figure or the original finished drawing and transferred this outline to the lithographic stone; in the printing process this image would naturally be reversed. In the process of completing this lithograph the artist chose to use subtler gradations in the smoke and shading, and finer lines for the flora, details that would have been lost in the poster medium. The context for this lithograph, like that of *Oncoming Storm: Adirondacks,* was defined by the times in which it was created. The instability of world peace by the fledgling Cold War was the concern of every citizen in this country and abroad. From air raid preparation in the classroom to the battles between President Truman and General MacArthur, to the turmoil at the 1968 Democratic National Convention, we were constantly reminded of the world powers' polar ideologies and how to address them.

Throughout Kent's artistic career he illustrated the emotion "troubled" repeatedly: *Foreboding* (Kent 1920, 125), *Lone Woman* (watercolor, Brooklyn Museum of Art), *Foreboding* and *And Women Must Weep* (lithographs), *Sorrows of the World* ("A Portfolio of Drawings" published by Schering Corporation), and the chapter head illustration "Brotherhood" (*It's Me O Lord*, 489), among them. He also brings this concept to his painting, *December Eight, 1941* (fig. 61).

Seen in the doorway of this painting are three female figures that represent pubescence, foreboding, and unyielding hope, and the girl at the fence, innocence; far down the road, almost out of sight,

we see a wayfaring young man carrying a few bare necessities. Of this composition, which Kent originally titled, *The Open Road*, he remarked: "The road that led out into a wider world has been open for many generations, and youth has taken it; and more youth now in these days will take it. And many, because of what will happen to them, will never return" (Kent 1942). Regardless of which title one applies to this painting, *The Open Road* or *December Eight, 1941* — the latter being a direct reference to the result of the bombing of Pearl Harbor — the story of love and loss remains evident. Obviously Kent's titles and his statement on the painting help

us better to understand his intentions, but, unlike some of his more ambiguous work, the message is quite clear without them. The devices that the artist employs are timeless. His use of figural positioning and color is standard and easily understood. The woman leaning into the portal — her left arm covering her face, her right

arm, raised in a gesture of emotional surrender, supports her weakened state — is undoubtedly the young man's mother. Her positioning against a clapboard house, and the implied reference to a male member of the family going off to war, were presaged by the image Kent created in his lithograph *And Women Must Weep* (fig. 62).

To her right, seated on the door steps, is her mother. A woman of age and experience, she has lived through this turmoil herself (her husband apparently is no longer with her), yet she clasps her hands out of unyielding hope. To their left stands a young woman adorned in the red of post-pubescence; she is one of two sisters. She leans against the house, clutching her own left arm in despair; she has lived long enough to have acquired some knowledge of the world and can understand the anxiety that her elders are experiencing. Her sister, seen at the

fence and dressed in the white of innocence, is too young and cannot. It is a vast world — here represented by the Adirondacks — that the young man enters into, with much peril that he must negotiate. Where the closed doorway may represent an ending, like that of the autumn which is upon them, the open second story window represents the anticipated return of spring, and hopefully the return of the young man.

The lithograph *Adirondack Cabin* (fig. 63) is another image that suggests love and loss, and

may, despite the acknowledged date of 1946, refer to loss due to the "Great War." Although the title aptly describes the locale, the lone female figure implies deeper meaning. Kent has rendered this figure from above her ankles, bringing her out of the domain of her Adirondack home and into the world of the viewer. The crossbars from the fence post are gone, further opening her world to us. The young woman appears to be in shock; her facial expression and posture are frozen. The disturbing letter that she has just read, she holds to her heart; the envelope she instinctively drops. By depicting a solitary figure surrounded by the Adirondack "wilderness," the artist is telling us that no one escaped the devastation of the war.

Kent's artwork during the period of the late 1930s and on through the next decade in particular provides us with a glimpse into the emotional difficulties war created for the artist. An abhorrence of violence was a fundamental belief of Kent's.[16] Whereas the execution of Sacco and Vanzetti by the State of Massachusetts in 1927 inspired Kent to produce his most graphic civil rights statements to date (oil portraits of severed heads), war manifested equally dramatic statements. A small oil referred to as *War* (1959) (fig. 64) depicts "Adam blasted to pieces and, in a sky lurid with flames, a bomber."[17] The scorched human torso retains enough muscle and bone to convey an expression of the pains and horrors of war.

With this in mind it becomes easier to comprehend the enormity of Kent's commitment to human rights, to social-democracy as a means of establishing social equality and progress, and his disgust for war and violence.

FIG. 64
War, 1959
Oil on board

Courtesy Joseph Erdelac Collection.

Therefore, when Fascism raised its viperous head in the Spanish Civil War, Kent struck back by providing the Loyalist cause with financial assistance and propaganda art. When the United States and other world powers refused to support the Loyalists, Fascism triumphed and gained a stronger foothold in Europe. In the aftermath, Kent, the Lincoln Brigade soldiers, and others like them, were discouraged and refused to have anything to do with the new battle (World War II).

Immediately following the Spanish Civil War Kent turned his enormous clout to the anti-war effort. It is believed that the com-

— a metaphor for the edge which Kent was about to cross over. We have seen this woman before, as the motherly character in *December Eight, 1941*, and *Hope Springs Eternal* (fig. 66).[18] These figures are heavy, muscular, sculpted, like the figures in Diego Rivera's *Figure Representing the Black Race* (1932, The Detroit Institute of Arts) and Picasso's *Large Bather* (1921–22, Musées Nationaux, Paris), and represent Kent's own struggles with relinquishing his hopes of peace, internally, and in the world theater. As Kent later recalled, "But in 1940, not even with Sally at my side, was the world — for me, for us, for anyone — that good" (Kent 1955, 535). For Kent, the final blow to peace was Hitler's invasion of the Soviet Union in June, 1941, which "opened a struggle between opposing ideologies." It was that war "that the believers in socialism, in loyalty to their beliefs and to democracy, now backed. From that time on it was, to me, our war" (Kent 1955, 542). Metaphorically, Kent leaps over the edge depicted in *At Peace* and back into the fight against Fascism; the painting *Wake Up, America!* (fig. 67) is representative of this monu-

FIGS. 65-66

At Peace, 1940
Oil on canvas

D. Wigmore Fine Art, Inc.

Hope Springs Eternal, 1941
Oil on canvas

Courtesy Rockwell Kent Papers,
Archives of American Art,
Smithsonian Institution.

position *At Peace* (fig. 65) was painted during this deceiving lull between wars. This full-figured, semi-reclined woman appears to be on top of the world and supposedly far from the pervasive troubles of the day. There is, however, an uneasiness that exudes from the painting. The clouds, like those depicted in *Oncoming Storm: Adirondacks*, are an omen of approaching trouble; they appear to be retreating from the area right of the composition. The woman is dressed in black, a color most often associated with grief or death; her expression is restless, not relaxed. What's more, a certain intensity is created by her proximity to the rocky ledge

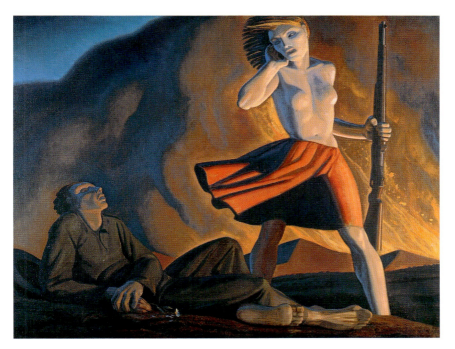

mental change in Kent's attitude toward war and symbolizes his decision to join the struggle.

The androgynous, Amazon-like figure in *Wake Up, America!* represents the spirit of war. This war against Fascism was not gender or racial or ethnically specific, it was, as Kent said, "our war." Kent had incorporated androgynous figures in his earlier work (including *Cromleagh, [Druid Sacrifice]*) but this "spirit of war" is a later model and appears to have its formalist origins in the 1938 Hugo LaFayette Black medal, *Life,*

Liberty and the Pursuit of Happiness (fig. 68). Like *Skaters* (fig. 50), *Asgaard in January* (fig. 9), and *Russian Mass* (fig. 70), *Wake Up, America!* developed from numerous pencil sketches and, in this case, a small gouache and transparent water-color study (fig. 69).

In content and in some respects, form, this figure is closely related to Kent's "Winged Victory" and *Our Seamen, Give 'Em A Hand* poster studies, and his *Fire!* (fig. 60) and *Eternal Vigilance is the Price of Liberty* lithographs. These works are propaganda art — promoting

FIGS. 67-69

Wake Up, America!, 1941
Oil on burlap

Major Vincent B. Murphy, Jr., U.S.M.C.

Life, Liberty, and the Pursuit of Happiness, 1938
Pencil on paper. Final cartoon for bronze medal.

Courtesy Rockwell Kent Papers, Archives of American Art, Smithsonian Institution.

Wake Up, America!, 1941 (study)
Gouache and watercolor on paper

Stanley Collection, Portland, Maine.

FIG. *70*

Russian Mass, 1928
Oil on canvas

Courtesy Steinway and Sons Art Collection,
Steinway Hall, New York.

the anti-fascism / pro-democracy cause — whose end goal is not unlike Norman Rockwell's *Four Freedoms:* freedom of speech, freedom to worship, freedom from want, freedom from fear. It should be noted that this propaganda art differs from the artist's three illustrations for *The New York Evening Call — Life and "Art"* (fig. 38), *Charity,* and *See No Evil, Hear No Evil, Speak No Evil* — which are blatantly pro-proletariat.[19]

Another symbolic figure that Kent includes in many of his compositions — paintings, drawings, prints, greeting cards, and so forth

— is the soaring figure, which he considered a "literal acceptance of a term of speech" (Kent 1955, 424). The figure depicted in *Russian Mass* (fig. 70), with its radiant diagonal light emanating from a sun-like source, illustrates the divine spirit portrayed in Sergei Rachmaninoff's score. "Music was in truth the voice of Life, with Life's supremely conscious being, Man, its instrument," Kent said (Kent 1955, 188). *Russian Mass* was the last of three commissions that Kent received from Steinway and Sons. The other two interpret Stravinsky's *The Fire Bird* and Wagner's *The Entrance of the Gods into Valhalla.*

Several preliminary pencil sketches for *Russian Mass* show an evolving horizontal figure that closely resembles the fully reclined model in Kent's wood engraving, *The Lovers,* also of 1928. The assembled worshippers and horse anticipate the artist's illustrations for Goethe's *Faust* (1941), Shakespeare's *Venus and Adonis* (1931), and the ceiling mural at the Cape Cinema (1930, Dennis, Massachusetts). The church is considered to be studio-created, as a similar structure does not exist in the immediate area of

FIG. 71-72

America, 1939

Oil on canvas

The Warner Library, Tarrytown,
New York. Gift of Rockwell Kent
in memory of his mother Sara
Holgate Kent.

Pastoral, 1941

Oil on canvas

Private Collection.

Asgaard Farm. The landscape in
the background does, however,
resemble the rolling Adirondack
foothills.

This interpretation of the
divine spirit through the compositional element light returns in
Kent's canvas, *America* (fig. 71).
Painted from virtually the same
vantage point as his "ode to love"
Pastoral (1941) (fig. 72), Kent portrays a frontier family bathed in
bold, diagonal sun rays emanating
from behind broken clouds. By
illustrating two settlers at work
outside their log cabin and the
vast horizon beyond, Kent is
making reference to the settling

of America, and as one could also interpret, to his deep American heritage as well as his own founding of Asgaard Farm. Kent purposefully contrasts the tiny cliffs-edge settlement against the vaster landscape to suggest the smallness of the physical in the all-encompassing spiritual; the sun's rays serve to heighten that affect. *America*, with its view of the setting sun — and essentially the view from Asgaard — has its antecedents in Thoreau's verse, "Every sunset which I witness inspires me with the desire to go to a West as distant and as fair as that into which the sun goes down. He appears to migrate westward daily, and tempt us to follow him. He is the Great Western Pioneer whom the nations follow."[20] In essence, *America* possesses the foundations of a luminist landscape — a subliminal spirituality created by the use of light and supportive structural elements — yet with a twentieth-century treatment, Kent's.

So we have come full circle. Through Kent's exploration of himself he has found the inspiration and the means — his art — by which to express his being. And through his canvases —

Untitled: Asgaard Farm (fig. 5), *Cloud Shadows* (fig. 36), their strong diagonal orientation toward his home — he has invited us to experience the same. Of art he has said, "Art is not art until it has effaced itself. Only when the blue paint of a sky ceases to be just color — becoming as it were the depths of space — is that blue right, and truly beautiful. Only when green becomes the growing grass, or the earth-colors land and rocks, when indigo becomes the ocean, and the colors of a figure become flesh and blood; only when words become ideas; when the sounds of music become images; only when every medium of the arts becomes transmuted into a portion of our living universe, only then is art consistent with the dignity of man" (Kent 1955, 137-138).

Notes

1. Irwin Edman, ed. (1951). *Essays by Ralph Waldo Emerson.* New York: Harper Colophon Books, 191.

2. Edman 1951, 255.

3. Rockwell Kent (1948). Stationery logo text.

4. Edman 1951, 251.

5. Luminism is a twentieth-century categorization of a predominantly nineteenth-century realist manner of treatment, in which atmospheric effect and spiritual emotion is conveyed by the use of stacked, overlapping modeled forms that recede to the horizon, and which contrast foreground detail against the often seamless tonal modulations of the sky.

6. Alfred Kazin and Daniel Aaron, eds. (1958). *Emerson: A Modern Anthology.* Boston: Houghton Mifflin, 97. Cited in Barbara Novak (1979). *American Painting of the Nineteenth Century, Realism, Idealism, and the American Experience.* New York: Harper & Row, Publishers, 123.

7. Edman 1951, 251.

8. The painting *Adirondacks* is but one composition that Kent painted on this theme. Another painting, also entitled *Adirondacks* (private collection), and two others, *Old Man, Old Horse, Old Barn, Old Mountains: Adirondacks* (Kiev Museum), and *And this, my child, is where your mother was born* (The Rockwell Kent

Gallery), continue his theme on the human condition.

9. Royal Cortissoz (1942). "Rockwell Kent and Divers Others." *New York Herald Tribune*, 8 February, section VI, 8. Kent's painting *This Is My Own* was one of the paintings that Cortissoz was referring to in this description. Cortissoz also thought that the "modest ascent in scale" of this painting and *December Eight, 1941* gave the painter "a greater luminosity." It is also interesting to note that Kent reworked *This Is My Own* to reflect the lengthening of the barn and the addition of a silo to increase his dairy production during World War II.

10. Elizabeth Hayt (1998). "In an Era of Humanoid Art, A Forerunner Finds a Place." *New York Times*, 13 December, 35 and 39.

11. Edman 1951, 390.

12. Ibid., 387.

13. Sally Kent (1943). "America Fêtes Soviet Students." *Fraternal Outlook* 5, no. 2 (February-March): 6-7, 25.

14. Rita Reif (1996). "Posters that once Stirred a Nation." *New York Times*, 25 February, 39. Kent had received numerous Soviet posters and anti-Nazi cartoons from the Soviet Consulate during the 1940s; the purpose of which was to distribute them to agencies in the United States and Canada that would exhibit them and therefore promote anti-Nazism and Russian War Relief.

15. The illustration — without text — for this poster, is pictured on page 543 of *It's Me O Lord* and is referred to on page 146 of Dan Burne Jones (1975). *The Prints of Rockwell Kent.*

16. Kent discusses his abhorrence of violence and war in several formats including in *It's Me O Lord* (318, 487, and 541, for example), in a 12 September 1957 interview with John Wingate of WABD in New York City, and in Carl Harris's 13 September 1940 *Daily Worker* article, "Artists Oppose Conscription and War, Says Rockwell Kent."

17. In a 7 July 1959 letter to Jacquie and Dan Burne Jones, Kent writes that he had been "making drawings for a book calling for an end to atomic test and war — a book on peace…I had sold them on the idea of using Michaelangelo's 'Creation of Man' [Stanley Collection] on the cover, with a line or two of text from the Book of Genesis, and on the back cover a painting of the same scene with Adam blasted to pieces."

18. *Hope Springs Eternal* depicts an Adirondack landscape surrounding a foreboding woman and carefree child. A similar painting, *Lone Woman* (private collection), depicts Monhegan and Manana Islands in Maine, and the carefree child has been painted over. With the use of ultraviolet light and X rays, the child in *Lone Woman* is seen clearly, but other former elements of this painting are not.

Some of the faint lines of underpaint imply mountains and a structure which suggest that Kent may have over-painted *Hope Springs Eternal* with the new composition *Lone Woman*. During the 1950s Kent's relationship with the Farnsworth Museum of Art in Rockland, Maine, soured when they suddenly retracted on their offer to host an exhibition of Kent's work, and ultimately, rejected Kent's gift of his "Great Kent Collection" (see *Rockwell Kent's Forgotten Landscapes*).

19. *Life and "Art"* appears on page 1 of the 16 February 1909 issue of *The New York Evening Call; Charity* on page 6 of the 11 March 1909 issue; and *See No Evil, Hear No Evil, Speak No Evil* on page 8 of the 3 April 1909 issue.

20. Jeffrey L. Duncan, ed. (1972). *Thoreau: The Major Essays*, 205, cited in John Wilmerding (1991). *American Views: Essays on American Art*. Princeton: Princeton University Press, 69.

FIG. *73* *Forest Ranger*, ca. 1943
Illustration for P. O. N. (Pride of Newark)
Beer advertisement. Private Collection.

FIG. *74* *Indian Corn*, ca. 1946–50
Pencil drawing for jewelry design.
The Rockwell Kent Gallery, Plattsburgh Art Museum.

Rockwell Kent: Selected Checklist of Adirondack Works

Scott R. Ferris

During his years as a painter, Rockwell Kent produced a vast number of oil paintings based, in whole and in part, on the Adirondack landscape. Some of these paintings began as oil studies, or as studies rendered in other media including watercolor, tempera, gouache, pencil, and pen. Others were conceived, developed, and completed on one canvas or board. The longest section in this checklist is devoted to Kent's Adirondack paintings. Works are arranged accordingly:

1) Oil paintings, studies, and related works,
    a) Adirondack landscapes,
    b) Composites,
2) Books,
3) Drawings and prints,
    a) Drawings for illustrations,
    b) Other drawings,
    c) Prints.

Individual entries in each section are arranged alphabetically by title. The artist did not develop a consistent manner of titling these works — many of them are similar in composition and title — which has led to considerable confusion when one attempts to identify individual objects. Quite often Kent would re-title a painting once he had already documented it under a different title. At other times he would title a painting, rework it, and either keep the same title or re-title it. He also left paintings untitled, especially if they were not scheduled for exhibition, or he would suggest to a new owner of a given work that they title it themselves.

Where there is more than one title for any given work, the first title listed is that which is known to have derived from the artist or his estate, or is a title which has long since been applied to a work and therefore has become the acknowledged standard. Original titles — whether they were changed by the artist or someone else at a later time — which are no longer regarded as the standard, are noted as being the original title.

Kent spelled the name "Au Sable," which may refer to a river, valley, or village, two ways: Au Sable and Ausable. His spellings have not been changed.

Names for some institutions that own more than one Adirondack work have been shortened for space considerations. These are:

Adirondack Museum. The Adirondack Museum, Blue Mountain Lake, N. Y.
Dilijan Museum. Dilijan Regional Museum, Dilijan, Republic of Armenia.
Gorki Museum. Gorki Museum, Moscow, Russia.
The Hermitage. The State Hermitage Museum, St. Petersburg, Russia.
Kiev Museum. Kiev Museum of Western and Eastern Art, Kiev, Republic of the Ukraine.
National Gallery of Armenia. National Gallery of Armenia, Yerevan, Republic of Armenia.
Odessa Museum. Odessa Museum of Western

and Eastern Art, Odessa, Republic of the Ukraine.
Pushkin Museum. Pushkin State Museum of Fine Arts, Moscow, Russia.
Rockwell Kent Gallery. The Rockwell Kent Gallery, Plattsburgh Art Museum, State University of New York, College at Plattsburgh.

The last line of each entry in the checklist contains a three segment catalogue number that relates to the author's catalogue raisonné categorization system. This system is laid out by the author's initials (SRF), followed by a geographical or generic abbreviation (e.g. ADK = Adirondacks, or MIS = Miscellaneous), followed by a numerical sequence which defines the alphabetical arrangement of object titles. Whole numbers refer to the sequence in which a specific entry generally appears in the catalogue raisonné, a decimal refers to a later entry, and a letter following a whole number, refers to an entry within a series.

Many works created by Kent have striking and often confusing similarities, due to his use of the same perspective or general geographic location from which he worked, or due to his use of a common theme. Hence the author has noted paintings with similar characteristics according to the following categories:

Geography. Refers to the geographic location at which a composition was conceived and/or rendered. The compositions portrayed may vary in manner of treatment, but the physical site depicted is recognizable and therefore comparable to another from the same area.

Perspective. Refers to the vantage point from which the artist rendered a specific composition. Atmospheric changes may be depicted in related works but the layout of the composition is virtually the same when compared with like canvases.

Theme. Refers to the context of the composition or the story-line that is created by the visual imagery.

What follows is a selected checklist of Kent's Adirondack works. A complete catalogue of Kent's works will be forthcoming.

Note: Work that appeared in the exhibit "The View from Asgaard: Rockwell Kent's Adirondack Legacy" (1999–2000) is designated by ✥.

Oil Paintings — Adirondack Landscapes
Including Studies and Related Works

Abandoned Farm, Adirondacks,
a.k.a. *Abandoned Farm,* ca. 1952
Oil on canvas, 34 1/8 x 44 in. / 87.3 x 111.8 cm.
Signed lower left and lower right
Rockwell Kent Gallery.
SRF-ADK-1.

Abandoned Home, 1956
Oil on canvas, 24 x 30 in. / 60.9 x 76.2 cm.
Other details under research.
SRF-ADK-2.

Adirondack Autumn,
a.k.a. *Adirondack Fall,*
a.k.a. *View from Asgaard, Fall,* 1951
Oil on canvas, 28 x 44 in. / 71.1 x 111.8 cm.
Signed lower right
Odessa Museum.
Originally in the collection of The Hermitage.
Given by that institution to the Odessa Museum
in 1975.
SRF-ADK-3.
Works related by geography and perspective: SRF-ADK-32,
71 and 90.

Adirondack Fall,
a.k.a. *Adirondack Splendor,*
a.k.a. *Fall Splendor,* ca. 1955
Oil on canvas, 20 x 24 in. / 50.8 x 60.9 cm.
Signed lower right
Private Collection.
SRF-ADK-4.
Works related by geography: SRF-ADK-33 and 58.

Adirondack Farm: Winter,
a.k.a. *Adirondack Farm,*
a.k.a. *Evening Red, Asgaard,* ca. 1959
Oil on canvas, 34 x 44 in. / 86.4 x 111.8 cm.
Signed lower right
Pushkin Museum.
See *Rockwell Kent's Forgotten Landscapes,* page 92,
for clarification of the use of third title.
SRF-ADK-5.
Works related by geography: SRF-ADK-96,
and perspective: SRF-ADK-17.

Adirondack Landscape, ca. late 1930s–40s
Oil on canvas mounted on plywood, 34 x 44 in. /
86.3 x 111.7 cm.
Unsigned, authenticated by Kent's second wife,
Frances, on the verso
Private Collection.
SRF-ADK-6.

Adirondack Spring,
a.k.a. *Adirondack Landscape,*
a.k.a. *Landscape,* ca. 1960–61
Oil on canvas, 28 x 34 in. / 71.2 x 86.5 cm.
Signed lower right
Samuel P. Harn Museum of Art,
University of Florida, Gainesville, Fla.
SRF-ADK-7.

Adirondack Valley,
a.k.a. *Valley in the Adirondack Mountains,*
a.k.a. *Valley in the Mountains,* 1950
Oil on canvas, 28 x 44 in. / 71.1 x 111.8 cm.
Signed lower right
Ownership attributed to Pushkin Museum;
current location unknown.
SRF-ADK-8.
Works related by geography: SRF-ADK-43, 52, 67 and 101.

❖ *Adirondacks*, 1928–30
Oil on canvas, 38 3/8 x 54 3/8 in. /
97.5 x 138.1 cm.
Signed lower right and dated
Corcoran Gallery of Art, Museum Purchase,
William A. Clark Fund.
SRF-ADK-9.
Works related by geography and theme: SRF-ADK-10, 13 and 66.

Adirondacks, 1941
Oil on panel, 29 x 34 3/4 in. / 73.6 x 88.3 cm.
Signed lower right
Private Collection.
SRF-ADK-10.
Works related by geography and theme: SRF-ADK-9, 13 and 66.

❖ *America*, 1939
Oil on canvas, 34 x 52 in. / 86.4 x 132.1 cm.
Signed lower right and dated:
"© Rockwell Kent 1939"
Warner Library, Tarrytown, N.Y.
Gift of Rockwell Kent in memory of his mother,
Sara Holgate Kent.
SRF-ADK-11.
Works related by geography and perspective: SRF-ADK-69.

❖ *Ancient Elm*, ca. 1961–62
Oil on canvas, 38 x 44 in. / 96.5 x 111.8 cm.
Signed lower right
Private Collection.
SRF-ADK-12.
Works related by geography: SRF-ADK-44.

And this, my child, is where your mother was born,
a.k.a. *And this my child is where you were born*,
1930, reworked 1950
Oil on canvas mounted on panel, 34 1/4 x 44 in. /
86.9 x 111.8 cm.
Signed lower right
Rockwell Kent Gallery.
SRF-ADK-13.
Works related by geography and theme: SRF-ADK-9, 10 and 66.

The Artist's Farm, Adirondacks, Jay, New York,
a.k.a. *Artist's Farm, Adirondacks, Au Sable Forks,
New York*, ca. 1950
Oil on canvas, 28 x 34 in. / 71.1 x 86.4 cm.
Signed lower right
The Rockwell Kent Legacies.
SRF-ADK-14.

Asgaard Barn, Morning,
a.k.a. *Asgaard Barn*, ca. 1956
Oil on canvas, 23 1/2 x 28 1/2 in. /
59.7 x 72.4 cm.
Signed lower right
Private Collection.
SRF-ADK-16.

Asgaard – Cloud Shadows, 1939
Oil on canvas, 28 x 38 in. / 71.1 x 96.5 cm.
Signed lower right
Bowdoin College Museum of Art, Brunswick, Me.
SRF-ADK-17.
Works related by geography: SRF-ADK-96,
and perspective: SRF-ADK-5.

Asgaard Cornfield,
mistitled *Asgaard Cornfield, California,*
originally titled, *Corn and Oats, Gray Day,* 1945
Oil on canvas, 28 x 44 in. / 71.1 x 111.8 cm.
Signed lower right
Collection, SBC Communications Inc.,
St. Louis, Mo.
SRF-ADK-18.
Works related by geography and perspective: SRF-ADK-61.

Asgaard Farm,
a.k.a. *Kent Home: Asgaard,* ca. 1940
Oil on canvas, 20 x 24 in. / 50.8 x 60.9 cm.
Signed lower right
Private Collection,
formerly the Collection of Hans Hinrichs.
SRF-ADK-19.
Works related by perspective and theme: SRF-ADK-49.

Asgaard from the Upper Road, ca. 1950
Oil on canvas, 28 x 44 in. / 71.1 x 111.8 cm.
Signed lower right
Private Collection.
SRF-ADK-20.
Works related by geography and perspective:
SRF-ADK-73, 102 and 105.

❖ *Asgaard in January,*
a.k.a. *Winter Afternoon,*
originally titled *Home from School, Asgaard,* 1958
Oil on canvas, 28 x 44 in. / 71.1 x 111.8 cm.
Signed lower right
F. B. Horowitz Fine Art, Ltd., Hopkins, Minn.
SRF-ADK-21.
Works related by geography and theme: SRF-ADK-107 and 80.

Asgaard Jerseys, 1965
Oil on canvas, 34 3/4 x 44 1/2 in. /
88.3 x 113 cm.
Signed lower right
Rockwell Kent Gallery.
SRF-ADK-22.
Works related by geography: SRF-ADK-37, 53 and 95.

Asgaard October, 1955
Oil on canvas, 28 x 34 in. / 71.1 x 86.4 cm.
Signed lower right
Kennedy Galleries, New York, N. Y.
SRF-ADK-23.
Works related by geography and perspective: SRF-ADK-38,
50 and 92.

Asgaard Winter, 1966
Oil on canvas, 34 1/2 x 42 in. / 87.5 x 106.6 cm.
Signed lower right
Private Collection.
SRF-ADK-24.
Works related by geography, perspective and theme:
SRF-ADK-94 and SRF-MIS-37.4.

❖ *Asgaard's Meadows,*
a.k.a. *Asgaard's Meadows (Adirondack Summer),*
a.k.a. *Asgaard,*
a.k.a. *Adirondack Summer,* 1945
Oil on canvas, 34 x 44 in. / 86.4 x 111.8 cm.
Signed lower right and dated
National Gallery of Armenia.
SRF-ADK-25.
Works related by geography: SRF-ADK-27 and 83.

Asgaard's Meadows, ca. 1950
Oil on canvas, 28 x 44 in. / 71.1 x 111.8 cm.
Signed lower right
Private Collection.
SRF-ADK-26.

Asgaard's Pastures,
a.k.a. *Asgaard's Pastures (Adirondacks)*, 1946
Oil on canvas, 28 x 44 in. / 71.1 x 111.8 cm.
Signed lower right
Attributed to Kiev Museum;
current location unknown.
SRF-ADK-27.
Works related by geography: SRF-ADK-25 and 83.

Au Sable Rapids: Adirondacks,
a.k.a. *Ausable River, Adirondacks*,
a.k.a. *Ausable River*,
a.k.a. *Rapids, Ausable River*, 1954
Oil on canvas, 34 x 44 in. / 86.4 x 111.8 cm.
Signed lower left
Pushkin Museum.
SRF-ADK-28.
Works related by geography: SRF-ADK-29 and 82.

❖ *Au Sable River Rapids*,
a.k.a. *Rapids, Ausable River*, 1950
Oil on canvas, 34 x 44 1/4 in. / 86.4 x 112.4 cm.
Signed lower right
Rockwell Kent Gallery.
SRF-ADK-29.
Works related by geography: SRF-ADK-28 and 82.

Au Sable River, Winter: Adirondacks,
a.k.a. *Au Sable River, Winter*,
a.k.a. *Ausable River, Winter (Adirondacks)*,
a.k.a. *The Ausable River in Winter*, 1960
Oil on canvas, 28 x 42 in. / 71.1 x 106.7 cm.
Signed lower left
The Hermitage.
SRF-ADK-30.

Au Sable River, Winter, ca. 1961–62
Oil on canvas, 23 x 28 in. / 58.5 x 71.1 cm.
Signed lower right
Flint Institute of Arts, Flint, Mich.
SRF-ADK-31.

Au Sable Valley, View of Whiteface, Fall, ca. 1955
Oil on canvas, 28 x 34 in. / 71.1 x 86.4 cm.
Signed lower right
The Rockwell Kent Legacies.
SRF-ADK-32.
Works related by geography and perspective: SRF-ADK-3,
71 and 90.

Autumn,
a.k.a. *Adirondack Landscape (I)*,
a.k.a. *Adirondack Landscape*, ca. 1955–62
Oil on panel, 20 x 24 in. / 50.8 x 60.9 cm.
Signed lower right
The Rockwell Kent Legacies.
SRF-ADK-33.
Works related by geography: SRF-ADK-4 and 58.

Birch Tree, ca. 1950s–60s
Oil on canvas, 24 x 30 in. / 60.9 x 76.2 cm.
Signed lower right
Private Collection.
SRF-ADK-35.
Works related by geography, perspective and theme: SRF-ADK-72.

❖ *Cloud Shadows*,
a.k.a. *Cloud Shadows (Asgaard)*, 1965
Oil on canvas, 34 x 44 in. / 86.4 x 111.8 cm.
Signed lower right
Robert Coleman Family Collection.
SRF-ADK-37.
Works related by geography: SRF-ADK-22, 53 and 95,
and perspective: SRF-ADK-53.

Clouds Over Asgaard, ca. 1955
Oil on canvas, 28 x 34 in. / 71.1 x 86.4 cm.
Signed lower right
Private Collection.
SRF-ADK-38.
Works related by geography and perspective: SRF-ADK-23,
50 and 92.

❖ *Clover Fields*,
a.k.a. *Clover Field*,
a.k.a. *Clover Fields, Asgaard*,
originally titled *In Clover*, 1939–40
Oil on canvas, 28 x 44 in. / 71.1 x 111.8 cm.
Signed lower left and lower right
Mead Art Museum, Amherst College,
Gift of Mrs. Robert A. Arms in memory
of Robert A. Arms (Class of 1927).
SRF-ADK-39.

The Covered Bridge at Jay,
a.k.a. *The Bridge at Jay, New York*,
a.k.a. *The Covered Bridge at Jay, New York*, ca. 1950
Oil on canvas board, 12 x 15 in. / 30.5 x 38.1 cm.
Unsigned
Private Collection.
This painting is a study for the oil, *Skaters*
(a.k.a. *The Covered Bridge at Jay*) (SRF-ADK-78).
SRF-ADK-39.1.

Creek in Winter,
a.k.a. *Creek in Winter, Asgaard Farm*, ca. 1940s–50s
Opaque watercolor on illustration board,
8 x 11 in. / 20.3 x 27.9 cm.
Signed lower left
Private Collection.
SRF-ADK-40.

Croquet Game, ca. 1956
Oil on canvas, 28 1/4 x 34 in. / 71.8 x 86.4 cm.
Signed lower right
Private Collection.
SRF-ADK-41.

Death of a Native: Adirondacks,
a.k.a. *Death of a Native*,
a.k.a. *Death of a Deer*, 1941
Oil on canvas mounted on masonite,
34 x 41 in. / 86.4 x 104.1 cm.
Signed lower left and right; dated and annotated
lower left: "1941/UOPWA 60 CIO/©"
"UOPWA" stands for the United Office and
Professional Workers of America; Kent had
been president of the Local 60. "CIO" stands
for Congress of Industrial Organizations.
Pushkin Museum.
Preliminary research suggests that this painting
was originally titled *Last Afternoon*.
SRF-ADK-42.

Deer on Palmer Hill,
a.k.a. *Palmer Hill, Adirondacks*, 1930
Oil on canvas, 28 x 34 in. / 71.1 x 86.4 cm.
Signed lower right
Private Collection.
SRF-ADK-43.
Works related by geography: SRF-ADK-8.

Elms (Stickney Bridge Road),
a.k.a. *Elms*,
a.k.a. *Tryst*, 1960
Oil on canvas, 34 x 44 in. / 86.4 x 111.8 cm.
Signed lower right
Private Collection.
SRF-ADK-44.
Works related by geography: SRF-ADK-12.

Elms on the Corner,
a.k.a. *The Meadow and Whiteface*, 1964
Oil on canvas, 28 x 44 in. / 71.1 x 111.8 cm.
Signed lower right
Private Collection.
SRF-ADK-45.

Evening Red (View from Asgaard),
a.k.a. *Red Sunset, Asgaard*,
a.k.a. *Red Sunset, View from Asgaard*, 1960
Oil on canvas, 34 x 44 in. / 86.4 x 111.8 cm.
Signed lower right
Pushkin Museum.
SRF-ADK- 46.
Works related by geography, theme and perspective:
SRF-ADK-103.1; by geography and theme: SRF-ADK-84 and 104.

"The Farm on Which I Live"
(direct translation from the Russian), 1965
Oil on canvas, 14 1/2 x 17 in. / 36.8 x 43.2 cm.
Signed lower right and inscribed,
"To my friends Vera and Yakov Tolchan"
The Tolchan Family Collection.
This painting may relate to *This Is My Own* or
The Artist's Farm, Adirondacks, Jay, New York. The
Tolchans were instrumental in producing the
1957 film of Kent's Soviet Union exhibition.
SRF-ADK-46.1.
Works related by theme: SRF-ADK-14, 87, 87a and SRF-MIS-36.1.

First Snow on Whiteface, 1956
Oil on canvas, 28 x 34 in. / 71.1 x 86.4 cm.
Signed lower right
Private Collection.
SRF-ADK-47.

❖ *Gladsheim*,
a.k.a. *Rockwell Kent's House*,
a.k.a. *Gladsheim, Asgaard Farm*,
a.k.a. *Kent Home: Asgaard*, 1963
Oil on board, 20 x 23 7/8 in. / 50.8 x 60.6 cm.
Signed lower right
Private Collection, formerly the Jacquie
and Dan Burne Jones Collection.
SRF-ADK-49.
Works related by perspective and theme: SRF-ADK-19.

Golden Fall, 1955
Oil on canvas, 28 x 34 in. / 71.1 x 86.4 cm.
Signed lower right
The Rockwell Kent Legacies.
SRF-ADK-50.
Works related by geography and perspective: SRF-ADK-23,
38 and 92.

Gorki House (Adirondacks),
a.k.a. *Gorki House in Keene*, 1962
Oil on canvas, 34 x 44 in. / 86.4 x 111.8 cm.
Gorki Museum.
This painting depicts the chalet at Summer Brook
Farm near Keene, N. Y., in which Maxim Gorki
stayed during his visit to the Adirondacks.
SRF-ADK-51.

Green Valley, ca. 1945
Oil on canvas, 28 x 44 in. / 71.1 x 111.8 cm.
Other details under research.
Illustrated facing page 456, *It's Me O Lord*.
SRF-ADK-52.
Works related by geography and perspective: SRF-ADK-67 and 101.

Hay Bales Evening,
a.k.a. *Hay Bales, Evening, Below Whiteface*, 1955
Oil on canvas, 34 1/4 x 44 1/8 in. /
86.9 x 112.1 cm.
Signed lower right
Collection Philip DeNormandie.
SRF-ADK-53.
Works related by geography: SRF-ADK-22, 37 and 95,
and perspective: SRF-ADK-37.

Haystack Farm, Au Sable Forks, N.Y., 1946
Oil on canvas, 28 x 44 in. / 70.5 x 111.8 cm.
Signed and dated lower right
Private Collection.
Commissioned from the artist by Seward Webb
("Pully") Pulitzer.
SRF-ADK-54.
Works related by geography, perspective and theme:
SRF-ADK-96.1a and 96.1b.

Home Again, ca. 1950s
Oil on canvas, 28 x 34 in. / 71.1 x 86.4 cm.
Signed lower right
Private Collection.
This painting was originally circa dated 1942–43,
perhaps reflective of the stylistic similarities to
paintings of that period. The inclusion of Kent's
dog, Gunnar, would probably date this work to
the later 1950s or early 1960s, or suggest that
the figures were added later.
SRF-ADK-55.

Horses in a Field, Roundup, Asgaard,
a.k.a. *Horses in Field (Roundup)*,
a.k.a. *Asgaard Roundup*,
a.k.a. *Asgaard – Horses*,
a.k.a. *Roundup*, ca. 1960
Oil on canvas, 28 x 44 in. / 71.1 x 111.8 cm.
Signed lower right
Private Collection.
SRF-ADK-56.
Works related by theme: SRF-ADK-91.

Kelly's Basin, Jay Mountain in the Adirondacks,
a.k.a. *Kelly's Basin, Jay Mountain*, ca. 1950s
Oil on canvas, 28 x 44 in. / 71.1 x 111.8 cm.
Signed lower right
Private Collection.
SRF-ADK-57.

Late Afternoon, ca. 1948
Oil on panel, 11 1/2 x 15 1/2 in. / 29.2 x 39.4 cm.
Signed lower right center
Georgia Museum of Art,
The University of Georgia, Athens, Ga.
This is a study for the larger canvas,
Sally on Horseback: Asgaard (SRF-ADK-76), minus
the figures and the finishing details. Based on
the original title of *Sally on Horseback — Asgaard
Morning (Sally on Nehru)* — the posthumous title,
Late Afternoon, would be inappropriate.
SRF-ADK-58.1.

Late Afternoon, 1955
Oil on panel, 11 1/4 x 15 1/4 in. / 28.6 x 38.7 cm.
Signed lower right
Private collection.
SRF-ADK-58.
Works related by geography: SRF-ADK-4 and 33.

Late Afternoon,
a.k.a. *Autumn*, 1955
Oil on canvas, 20 x 24 in. / 50.8 x 60.9 cm.
Signed lower right
The Rockwell Kent Legacies.
SRF-ADK-59.
Works related works by geography: SRF-ADK-70 and 85.

Lilacs,
a.k.a. *Dooryard Lilacs*, ca. 1968
Oil on canvas, 28 x 34 in. / 71.1 x 86.4 cm.
Signed lower right
Collection of Mr. and Mrs. Walter Dubay.
SRF-ADK-60.

Meadow and Cornfield,
originally titled *Corn and Oats, Blue Day*, 1945
Oil on burlap, 28 x 44 in. / 71.1 x 111.8 cm.
Signed lower right
Private Collection.
This painting has been reworked at least twice.
Once, to add clouds and a woman, child, and
frog that were in the foreground — this was done
by the artist; the second time to eliminate the
above mentioned elements — this was done
posthumously.
SRF-ADK-61.
Works related by geography and perspective: SRF-ADK-18.

Meadow and Whiteface,
a.k.a. *Whiteface and Meadow*, ca. 1966
Oil on canvas, 22 x 34 in. / 55.9 x 86.4 cm.
Signed lower right
Private Collection.
SRF-ADK-62.

Moonlight, Winter,
a.k.a. *Asgaard,*
a.k.a. *Moonlight*, ca. 1940
Oil on canvas, 28 x 34 in. / 71.1 x 86.4 cm.
Signed lower right
Whitney Museum of American Art,
New York, N.Y.
SRF-ADK-63.

Mount Whiteface,
a.k.a. *Mt. Whiteface — Asgaard*, 1961
Oil on board, 20 x 25 in. / 50.8 x 63.5 cm.
Signed lower right
Private Collection.
SRF-ADK-64.

❖ *Mountain Road*, ca. 1960
Oil on canvas, 28 x 44 in. / 71.1 x 111.8 cm.
Signed lower right
Adirondack Museum. 74.68.1 (356)
SRF-ADK-65.

Old Man, Old Horse, Old Barn,
Old Mountain: Adirondacks,
a.k.a. *Old Man, Old Horse, Old Barn,*
Old World, 1957
Oil on canvas, 34 x 44 in. / 86.4 x 111.8 cm.
Signed lower right
Kiev Museum.
This painting may have been titled *Time
and Eternity* prior to the addition of the old
man and horse.
SRF-ADK-66.
Works related by geography and theme: SRF-ADK-9, 10 and 13.

❖ *Oncoming Storm: Adirondacks,*
a.k.a. *Oncoming Storm,*
a.k.a. *Adirondack Valley,*
a.k.a. *Ausable Valley,*
originally titled *The Au Sable Valley,* 1946
Oil on canvas, 34 x 44 in. / 86.4 x 111.8 cm.
Signed lower right
National Gallery of Armenia.
SRF-ADK-67.
Works related by geography and perspective: SRF-ADK-52 and 101.

Once an Acorn, Once a Child,
formerly mistitled, *Oak Ridge Oak,* 1961
Oil on canvas, 34 x 44 in. / 86.4 x 111.8 cm.
Signed lower right
The Rockwell Kent Legacies.
Formerly believed to be an Oak Ridge, Va.,
landscape, thus the previous title of *Oak Ridge
Oak* and earlier date of 1956. There are
similarities between this scene and that depicted
in *Ancient Oak* and *Child Under Tree* (a.k.a. *Virginia,
Ancient Oak*); the former being a commanding
portrait of an oak tree, and in the latter, a
dominating oak with mannequin-like figures
on either side of the tree.
SRF-ADK-68.

Pastoral, 1941
Oil on canvas, 34 x 52 in. / 86.4 x 132.1 cm.
Signed, dated and annotated lower right:
"Rockwell Kent. U.A.A. 1941"
Private Collection.
"U.A.A." is an abbreviation for United American
Artists, a union of which Kent was a member.
SRF-ADK-69.
Works related by geography and perspective: SRF-ADK-11.

Picnic in the Pines,
a.k.a. *Sunset in the Pines,*
originally titled *Asgaard Pine Grove,* ca. 1956–68
Oil on canvas, 28 x 44 in. / 71.1 x 111.8 cm.
Signed lower right
Sally Kent Gorton.
After combing several references, the author has
discovered that there has been no consistency in
dating this painting. However, it is known that
the apparent study for this work, *Sunset Through the
Pines,* was given by the artist to Mrs. Dan Burne
"Jacquie" Jones in 1963 (believed to be the year
of the study). It is quite possible that Kent began
these two works as early as 1956 and completed
the larger canvas at a much later date.
SRF-ADK-70.
Works related by geography, perspective and theme: ADK-85,
and by geography: SRF-ADK-59.

❖ *Pine Tops and Mountain Peaks,*
a.k.a. *Tree Tops and Mountain Peaks,*
a.k.a., *Mountain Peaks and Tree Tops,* 1960
Oil on canvas, 34 x 44 in. / 86.4 x 111.8 cm.
Signed lower left and lower right
Mr. and Mrs. William M. E. Clarkson.
This painting is a prime example of the artist's
re-titling his work. The title *Pine Tops and Mountain
Peaks* is hand written by the artist on the back
of a photograph of this work. The title *Tree Tops
and Mountain Peaks* was typed on a small piece
of adhesive tape and applied to the back of the
upper stretcher bar. This second method of
labeling a painting was frequently used by Kent.
This second title was also used by Harbor Gallery
(formerly of Cold Spring Harbor and Manhattan,
N.Y.) in its 1966 exhibition brochure and in the
accompanying publicity. The title *Mountain Peaks*

and Tree Tops was used by Larcada Gallery (formerly of Manhattan; Kent's last gallery representative) in its publications. As there is nearly equal support for each of these titles, this author has chosen to favor Kent's own handwritten title. The double signature suggests that Kent touched up this painting at a later time.

To further complicate matters, another painting, referred to as *Tree Tops and Mountain Peaks* (SRF-ADK-90), depicts a very similar view of Whiteface Mountain from Asgaard. The current owner states that this second work was sold by Harbor Gallery during its 1966 Kent exhibition, later returned to the Gallery and then resold to him. Further confusion arises when these two paintings are compared with two similar works: *Au Sable Valley, View of Whiteface, Fall* (SRF-ADK-32), and *Adirondack Autumn* (SRF-ADK-3). The alternating foreground detail — depicting deciduous versus coniferous trees — and the variant artist's dates attributed to these paintings — from 1951 to the 1960s — immediately suggest that Kent has employed artistic license. This also suggests that it would be unwise to circa date a painting according to an object in a composition (trees, in this case).
SRF-ADK-71.

Works related by geography and perspective: SRF-ADK-3, 32 and 90.

Pines in the Snow, ca. 1960
Oil on artist board, 12 x 15 1/2 in. / 30.5 x 39.4 cm.
Signed lower right
Fairbanks Northstar Borough Library, Fairbanks, Alaska.
This painting is strikingly similar to *Snow Laden Pines* and therefore may have been a study for the same, yet the finished qualities of this painting suggest that it could have easily been an independent work.
SRF-ADK-71.1. See SRF-ADK-79.

River Bank with Birch Tree and Nude, a.k.a. *Birch Tree*, ca. 1950s–60s
Oil on canvas, 28 x 34 in. / 71.1 x 86.4 cm.
Unsigned
The Rockwell Kent Legacies.
This composition may not depict a river but the swimming hole at Asgaard Farm. The title *Birch Tree* is a title given by the artist to another, very similar painting, minus the nude figure (see *Birch Tree*).
SRF-ADK-72.

Works related by geography, perspective and theme: SRF-ADK-35.

The Road to Asgaard: Adirondacks, a.k.a. *The Road to Asgaard*, a.k.a. *The Road to Asgaard (Adirondacks)*, a.k.a. *Barns and Adirondack Mountains*, a.k.a. *Asgaard, Farm Home of the Kents*, 1960
Oil on canvas, 34 x 44 in. / 86.4 x 111.8 cm.
Signed lower right
The Hermitage.
SRF-ADK-73.

Works related by geography and perspective:
SRF-ADK-20, 102 and 105.

Rockwell Kent's Studio, ca. 1950–53
Oil on plywood, 12 x 16 in. / 30.5 x 40.6 cm.
Signed lower right
Destroyed by fire.
In the early 1980s Dan Burne Jones informed
the author that this painting had been a sketch
on which the artist applied some finishing
touches before selling it to Jacquie Jones, as
a gift to her husband, Dan.
SRF-ADK-74.

Works related by geography: SRF-ADK-108.

Sally and Gunnar, 1956
Oil on panel, 16 x 24 in. / 40.6 x 60.9 cm.
Inscribed lower right:
"Rockwell to Sally, March 21, 1956"
The Rockwell Kent Legacies.
Gunnar is the name given to the small terrier
owned by the Kents; March 21 is Sally's birthday.
SRF-ADK-75.

Sally on Horseback: Asgaard,
a.k.a. *Sally on Horseback*,
originally titled *Asgaard Morning*
(*Sally on Nehru*), 1948
Oil on canvas mounted on plywood, 34 x 44 in. /
86.4 x 111.8 cm.
Signed lower right
Pushkin Museum.
SRF-ADK-76.

Works related by geography and perspective: SRF-ADK-58.1.

❖ *Skaters*,
a.k.a. *The Covered Bridge at Jay*, 1950
Oil on canvas, 28 x 42 in. / 71.2 x 106.7 cm.
Signed lower right
Private Collection.
In a 23 March 1960 letter to the Dan Burne Jones
family, Sally Kent wrote, "There comes Rockwell
now — back from painting the covered bridge at
Jay." Sally may have been referring to this paint-
ing or to the above study, or she may have been
referring to another composition altogether.
SRF-ADK-78. See SRF-39.1.

Snow Laden Pines, ca. 1960–67
Oil on canvas, 28 x 34 in. / 71.1 x 86.4 cm.
Signed lower right
Private Collection.
SRF-ADK-79. See SRF-ADK-71.1.

The Snowman,
a.k.a. *Asgaard, Winter*,
originally titled, *Snow Man – Asgaard*, ca. 1962–63
Oil on canvas, 28 x 44 in. / 71.1 x 111.8 cm.
Signed lower right
Anchorage Historical and Fine Arts Museum,
Anchorage, Alaska.
SRF-ADK-80.

Works related by geography and theme: SRF-ADK-21 and 107.

Spring Freshet,
a.k.a. *View of the Ausable River,* 1945
Oil on canvas mounted on plywood, 20 x 24 in. /
50.8 x 60.9 cm.
Signed and dated lower left
Private Collection.
View of the Ausable River is a posthumous,
descriptive title whereas *Spring Freshet* was the
title the original purchasers gave the painting,
with the artist's consent.
SRF-ADK-82.

Works related by geography: SRF-ADK-28 and 29.

Summer Day: Asgaard,
a.k.a. *Adirondack Landscape (Asgaard),*
a.k.a. *Summer Day,*
a.k.a. *Summer Day: Asgaard (Adirondacks),*
a.k.a. *Asgaard Pasture,* ca. 1950
Oil on canvas, 34 x 44 in. / 86.4 x 111.8 cm.
Signed lower right
The Hermitage.
See *Rockwell Kent's Forgotten Landscapes,* p. 92,
for clarification of the use of the fifth title.
SRF-ADK-83.

Works related by geography: SRF-ADK-25 and 27.

Sunset in Winter, ca. 1964
Oil on panel, 12 x 16 in. / 30.5 x 40.6 cm.
Signed lower right and inscribed lower left:
"To my young friend Jim Rosenberg on his
90th birthday"
Private Collection.
SRF-ADK-84.

Works related by geography and theme: SRF-ADK-46,
103.1 and 104.

Sunset Through the Pines,
a.k.a. *Trees in the Kent Yard,* ca. 1963
Oil on canvas, 20 x 28 in. / 50.8 x 71.1 cm.
Signed lower right and inscribed,
"'To Jacquie, 1963.' RK"
Private Collection, formerly the Jacquie
and Dan Burne Jones Collection.
This painting appears to be a study for the
larger canvas, *Picnic in the Pines.*
SRF-ADK-85.

Works related by geography, perspective and theme: SRF-ADK-70,
and by geography: SRF-ADK-59.

This Is My Own,
a.k.a. *Meadows and Mountains,* 1940
Oil on canvas, 49 x 74 1/2 in. / 124.5 x 189.2 cm.
Signed lower right and annotated:
"Rockwell Kent U.O.P.W.A. 60 C.I.O. 1940"
Pushkin Museum.
SRF-ADK-87.

Works related by geography and perspective: SRF-ADK-87a and
SRF-MIS-36.1, and by theme: SRF-ADK-46.1.

❖ *This Is My Own,* ca. 1940
Oil on wood panel,
10 x 15 in. / 25.4 x 38.1 cm. (sight)
Signed lower right
Private Collection.
This painting is a study for the much larger oil
by the same title.
SRF-ADK-87a.

Works related by geography and perspective:
SRF-ADK-87 and SRF-MIS-36.1, and by theme: SRF-ADK-46.1.

Three Maidens, 1960
Oil on canvas, 34 x 44 in. / 86.4 x 111.8 cm.
Signed lower right
Private Collection.
SRF-ADK-89.

Tree Tops and Mountain Peaks, ca. 1950s
Oil on canvas, 28 x 34 in. / 71.1 x 86.4 cm.
Signed lower right
Robert Coleman Family Collection.
SRF-ADK-90.
Works related by geography and perspective: SRF-ADK-3, 32 and 71.

Untitled: Adirondack Corral, ca. 1950s–60s
Oil on canvas, 28 x 44 in. / 71.1 x 111.8 cm.
Signed lower right
Private Collection.
SRF-ADK-91.
Works related by theme: SRF-ADK-56.

Untitled: Adirondack Landscape, ca. 1960
Oil on panel, 12 x 16 in. / 30.5 x 40.6 cm.
Signed lower right and inscribed lower left:
"To our dear friend, Larissa – S & R."
Private Collection.
This painting is the second of two with ties to the Soviet Union that came on the auction block in the United States during the 1990s. The first painting, referred to as *Russian Landscape, Barvikha*, was painted in the USSR. This second painting, referred to as Untitled: Adirondack Landscape, may have been a study for *Asgaard October* (SRF-ADK-23). It was given by the Kents to their Russian interpreter and friend, Larissa Alushkina, in 1960 (see *Rockwell Kent's Forgotten Landscapes*, p. 75).
SRF-ADK-92.
Works related by geography and perspective: SRF-ADK-23, 38 and 50.

Untitled: Adirondack Landscape, ca. 1950s
Oil on panel, 12 x 16 in. / 30.5 x 40.6 cm.
Signed lower left
Private Collection.
SRF-ADK-93.

Untitled: Asgaard Barn, Winter, ca. 1959–60
Oil on masonite, 19 1/2 x 22 1/2 in. / 49.5 x 57.2 cm.
Signed lower right
Rose Art Museum, Brandeis University, Waltham, Mass.
The similarity of this piece to *Asgaard Winter* (SRF-ADK-24) suggests that it may have been a study for the larger canvas.
SRF-ADK-94.
Works related by geography, perspective and theme: SRF-ADK-24 and SRF-MIS-37.4.

❖ Untitled: Asgaard Farm,
a.k.a. Untitled: Ausable Farm,
a.k.a. *Au Sable Valley Farm*, ca. 1961
Oil on canvas, 28 x 42 in. / 71.1 x 106.7 cm.
Signed lower right
Adirondack Museum. 61.56.1 (44)
SRF-ADK-95.
Works related by geography: SRF-ADK-22, 37 and 53.

Untitled: Asgaard Farm, ca. 1950s
Oil on board, 12 x 16 in. / 30.5 x 40.6 cm.
Signed lower right
Private Collection.
SRF-ADK-96.
Works related by geography: SRF-ADK-5 and 17.

Untitled: Haystack Farm, autumn study, ca. 1946
Oil on pine board, 11 1/2 x 16 in. /
29.2 x 40.6 cm.
Signed lower right
Private Collection.
According to the owner of this painting, who purchased it directly from Kent, this is one of four seasonal views depicting the Whiteface range. The other two alleged paintings have yet to be documented.
SRF-ADK-96.1a.
Works related by geography, perspective and theme:
SRF-ADK-54 and 96.1b.

Untitled: Haystack Farm,
late summer study, ca. 1946
Oil on masonite, 12 x 16 in. / 30.5 x 40.6 cm.
Signed lower right
Private Collection.
SRF-ADK-96.1b.
Works related by geography, perspective and theme:
SRF-ADK-54 and 96.1a.

Untitled: In the Adirondacks, ca. 1940s–50s
Oil on canvas, 24 x 30 in. / 61.2 x 76.9 cm.
Signed lower right
Private Collection.
SRF-ADK-99.

Untitled: View from Palmer Hill,
a.k.a. *From Palmer Hill*, ca. 1950
Oil on canvas, 28 x 44 in. / 71.1 x 111.8 cm.
Signed lower left and inscribed:
"To Albert and Riette / Rockwell Kent"
Private Collection.
Albert and Riette Kahn were close personal friends of the Kents as well as political allies of the artist. Palmer Hill, just north of the village of Au Sable Forks, was a favorite picnicking spot of the Kents.
SRF-ADK-101.
Related works by geography and perspective: SRF-ADK-52 and 67.

Upper Road to Asgaard, a.k.a. *Asgaard Farm*, ca. 1958
Oil on panel, 20 x 24 in. / 50.8 x 61 cm.
Signed lower left
Private Collection.
SRF-ADK-102.
Works related by geography and perspective: SRF-ADK-20, 73 and 105.

Whiteface Mountain Under Clouds: Adirondacks,
a.k.a. *Whiteface Mountain Under Clouds*,
a.k.a. *Whiteface in Cloud (Adirondacks)*, 1952
Oil on canvas, 34 x 44 in. / 86.4 x 111.8 cm.
Signed lower right
Kiev Museum.
SRF-ADK-103.

Whiteface Sunset, 1960
Oil on canvas board, 9 x 12 in. / 22.9 x 30.5 cm.
Unsigned, inscribed on verso by artist:
"To Sally. — Even more beautiful than the
morning. To my beloved on our twentieth
anniversary. R."
Sally Kent Gorton.
This painting is a study for the larger canvas,
Evening Red (View from Asgaard).
SRF-ADK-103.1.
Works related by geography, theme and perspective: SRF-ADK-46,
and by geography and theme: SRF-ADK-84 and 104.

Whiteface Sunset, ca. late 1960s–70
Oil on canvas, 20 x 25 in. / 50.8 x 63.5 cm.
Signed lower right
Private Collection.
SRF-ADK-104.
Works related by geography and theme: SRF-ADK-46,
103.1 and 84.

Winter Evening: Asgaard, 1959
Oil on canvas, 28 x 44 in. / 71.1 x 111.8 cm.
Signed lower right
Dilijan Museum.
SRF-ADK-105.
Works related by geography and perspective: SRF-ADK-20,
73 and 102.

✣ *Winter Sunrise, Whiteface Mountain*,
a.k.a. *Winter Sunrise, Whiteface, Asgaard*,
ca. 1952–60
Oil on canvas mounted on masonite,
28 x 44 in. / 71.1 x 111.8 cm.
Signed lower right
John Horton Collection.
SRF-ADK-106. See SRF-ADK-106a.

Winter Sunrise,
a.k.a. *Winter Sunrise, Adirondacks*, 1952
Oil on panel, 11 1/2 x 16 in. / 29.2 x 40.6 cm.
Signed and inscribed lower left:
"Rockwell to Sally, Mar. 21, 1952"
Given by Kent to his wife Sally on her birthday.
Sally Kent Gorton.
This painting is a study for *Winter Sunrise,
Whiteface Mountain*.
SRF-ADK-106a. See SRF-ADK-106.

Woman and Child on way to Barn, ca. 1966
Oil on canvas, 34 x 42 in. / 86.4 x 106.7 cm.
Signed lower right
The Rockwell Kent Legacies.
The choppy descriptiveness of this title is an
example of some of the later posthumous titling.
SRF-ADK-107.
Works related by geography and theme: SRF-ADK-21 and 80.

Woodsman,
a.k.a. *Woodcutter*,
a.k.a. *Carrying Wood, Adirondacks*, late 1960s–70
Oil on canvas, 20 x 24 in. / 50.8 x 60.9 cm.
Signed lower right
The Rockwell Kent Legacies.
In 1982 the author was informed by Kent's
widow, Sally Kent Gorton, that this painting
is believed to be the artist's last completed oil.
SRF-ADK-108.
Works related by geography: SRF-ADK-74.

Young Pines and Old Hills, 1950
Oil on canvas, 23 x 28 in. / 58.4 x 71.1 cm.
Signed lower right
The Rockwell Kent Legacies.
SRF-ADK-109.

Oil Paintings — Composites
Including Studies and Related Works

Asgaard Christmas Tree, 1954
Oil on panel, 12 1/4 x 16 1/2 in. / 31.1 x 41.9 cm.
Inscribed lower right: "XX"
The Rockwell Kent Legacies.
According to John Gorton (late second husband
of Sally Kent Gorton and former director of The
Rockwell Kent Legacies), the inscription "XX"
was "uncharacteristically" used by Kent as a
signature for greeting card company commissions
during the height of the McCarthy era.
SRF-MIS-2.
Works related by theme: SRF-MIS-9, 10, 12, 13, 37.2, 37.3,
40 and 40a.

✥ *At Peace*, 1940
Oil on canvas, 28 x 44 in. / 71.1 x 111.8 cm.
Signed lower right
D. Wigmore Fine Art, Inc., New York, N.Y.
SRF-MIS-4.

Bituminous Coal Series using the
Adirondack landscape:
These three paintings represent some of the
images used by Bituminous Coal Institute for
an advertising campaign conducted during 1945
and 1946. This commission was arranged by
the New York City advertising firm, Benton
and Bowles, Inc.

Power…for the Wheels of Progress, 1945
Oil on canvas, 38 x 44 in. / 96.5 x 111.8 cm.
Signed lower left
Palmer Museum of Art, The Pennsylvania State
University, University Park, Penn.
SRF-MIS-6a.

To Make Dreams Come True, 1946
Oil on canvas, 38 x 44 in. / 96.5 x 111.8 cm.
Unsigned
College of Engineering and Mineral Resources,
West Virginia University,
Morgantown, W. Va.
SRF-MIS-6f.

Might…to Move Mountains, 1946
Oil on canvas, 36 x 42 in. / 91.4 x 106.7cm.
Signed lower right
University of Missouri School of Mines,
Rolla, Mo.
SRF-MIS-6h.

Christmas, 1954
Oil on panel, 12 1/8 x 16 1/8 in. / 30.8 x 40.9 cm.
Inscribed lower left: "XX"
The Rockwell Kent Legacies.
SRF-MIS-9.
Works related by theme: SRF-MIS-2, 10, 12, 13, 37.2, 37.3,
40 and 40a. See SRF-MIS-2 regarding signature.

Christmas Eve, ca. 1950
Opaque watercolor on illustration board,
8 3/4 x 10 1/4 in. / 22.2 x 26 cm.
Signed lower left
Private Collection.
American Artists Group greeting card No. 25 B 18.
SRF-MIS-10.
Works related by theme: SRF-MIS-2, 9, 12, 13, 37.2, 37.3,
40 and 40a.

❖ *Christmas Tree*, ca. 1951
Oil on canvas board, 12 x 16 in. / 30.5 x 40.6 cm.
Signed lower right
James and Charlene James Duguid.
American Artists Group greeting card
No. 15 B 90.
SRF-MIS-12.
Works related by theme: SRF-MIS-2, 9, 10, 12, 37.2, 37.3,
40 and 40a.

City Lights at Christmas,
a.k.a. *Christmas Eve*, ca. 1944–46
Gouache and watercolor on paper,
12 x 14 1/2 in. / 30.5 x 36.8 cm.
Unsigned
Private Collection.
SRF-MIS-13.
Works related by theme: SRF-MIS 2, 9, 10, 12, 37.2, 37.3,
40 and 40a.

❖ *December Eight*, 1941,
originally titled *The Open Road*, 1941
Oil on canvas, 43 1/2 x 70 1/4 in. /
110.5 x 178.4 cm.
Signed lower right and annotated:
"© Rockwell Kent U.A.A. 1941"
Rockwell Kent Gallery.
The artist intentionally re-titled this painting
to acknowledge the bombing of Pearl Harbor,
Hawaii, by the Japanese on 7 December 1941,
and the entry of the United States into World
War II.
SRF-MIS-15.

Heavy, Heavy Hangs Over Thy Head,
originally titled, *Heavy, Heavy*, ca. 1946–49
Oil on canvas, 28 x 34 in. / 71.1 x 86.4 cm.
Signed lower right with copyright symbol
Baltimore Museum of Art.
The text, "Heavy, Heavy Hangs Over Thy
Head," appears within the lower section of
the composition.
SRF-MIS-18.

Hope Springs Eternal, 1941
Oil on canvas, 34 x 44 in. / 86.4 x 111.8 cm.
Signed lower right and annotated:
"Rockwell Kent UOPWA 60/1941 CIO"
Location unknown. Other details under research.
SRF-MIS-19.

On Earth Peace, 1944
Oil, mural, 15 x 12 feet / 4.6 x 3.7 m.
Signed lower right with copyright symbol
Wall niche in the Committee on Merchant
Marine and Fisheries hearing room, Longworth
House Office Building, Washington, D.C. This
mural was originally rendered for the House
Committee on Interstate and Foreign Commerce.
Kent depicted his own farm, Asgaard, in the
lower left corner of the mural. His wife, Sally,
served as the model for the angels; the profile of
the angel's head (left) was also used in *Portrait of
Sally* (see SRF-MIS-31). A similar landscape was used
in a Christmas card design for subscribers of *Life*
magazine in 1945 (6 1/2 x 9 3/4 in., with envelope). The text, "On Earth Peace," appears above,
in the arch of the niche.
SRF-MIS-23.

❖ *Russian Mass*, a.k.a. *Russian Mass,*
  Au Sable Forks, New York, 1928
  Oil on canvas, 34 1/4 x 44 1/2 in. /
  87.6 x 113 cm.
  Signed lower right and dated
  Steinway & Sons, New York, N.Y.
  SRF-MIS-28.

❖ *Sally,*
  a.k.a. *Portrait of Sally*, ca. 1944–49
  Oil on board, 20 x 24 in. / 50.8 x 60.9 cm.
  Unsigned
  Rockwell Kent Gallery.
  SRF-MIS-31.

  This Is My Own, ca. 1940–42
  Reverse painting on glass, 10 x 21 1/2 in. /
  25.4 x 54.6 cm.
  Unsigned
  Artwork for the header to a larger vertical,
  wood-framed mirror. Given the fact that the
  composition of this painting is a slight variation
  on SRF-ADK-87 and 87a above, the author has
  assigned it the same title.
  The Rockwell Kent Legacies.
  SRF-MIS-36.1.

  Works related by geography and perspective: SRF-ADK-87 and 87a,
  and by theme: SRF-ADK-46.1.

  Untitled: Boy Running with Kite, ca. 1940–42
  Oil on panel, 2 1/2 x 3 in. / 6.4 x 7.6 cm.
  Picture frame — painted with a lighthearted
  self portrait — framing a childhood photograph
  of the artist.
  The Rockwell Kent Legacies.
  SRF-MIS-37.1.

  Works related by theme: SRF-MIS-37.5.

  Untitled: Christmas Evening, ca. 1946
  Oil on canvas board, 10 1/2 x 14 1/2 in. /
  26.7 x 36.8 cm.
  Signed lower left
  Private Collection.
  Because of its similarity to the painting *Winter
  Evening* (SRF-MIS-40), it is assumed that this work
  was also intended for use in a General Electric
  annual calendar and perhaps a Christmas card.
  Though contrary to Kent's statement (see *Winter
  Evening*, below), it has been suggested that this
  painting depicts a location between Bethel and
  East Granville, Vermont.
  SRF-MIS-37.2.

  Works related by geography: SRF-MIS-40,
  and by theme: SRF-MIS-2, 9, 10, 12, 13, 37.2, 40 and 40a.

❖ Untitled: Christmas scene in *Country Gentleman*, 1943
  Oil on canvas, dimensions unknown
  Signed lower right
  Location unknown. Other details under research.
  Used as the cover illustration for the December
  issue of *Country Gentleman* and as a Christmas card
  from this company to its subscribers.
  SRF-MIS-37.3.

  Works related by theme: SRF-MIS-2, 9, 10, 12, 13, 37.2, 40 and 40a.

❖ Untitled: "1947 / Asgaard," 1947
  Painted wood blanket or storage chest,
  19 x 25 x 18 1/2 in. / 48.3 x 63.5 x 46.9 cm.
  "1947 / Asgaard" inscribed on lid of chest,
  surrounding a scene of the Asgaard barn in winter
  (see *Asgaard Winter* SRF-ADK-24); one of several
  functional pieces made for home use by the artist.
  Adirondack Museum. 99.11.1
  SRF-MIS-37.4.

  Works related by geography, perspective
  and theme: SRF-ADK-24 and 94.

Untitled: Nude Girl and Bird, ca. 1940–42
Oil on panel, 2 1/2 x 3 in. / 6.4 x 7.6 cm.
Picture frame — painted with a lighthearted
depiction of Kent's third wife — around a
childhood photograph of Sally Kent Gorton.
The Rockwell Kent Legacies.
SRF-MIS-37.5.
Works related by theme: SRF-MIS-37.1.

✥ *Wake Up, America!*,
originally titled *Wake Up!*, 1941
Oil on burlap, 34 x 44 in. / 86.4 x 111.8 cm.
Signed lower right and annotated:
"© Rockwell Kent U.A.A. 1941"
Major Vincent B. Murphy, Jr., U.S.M.C.
SRF-MIS-39. See SRF-MIS-39a.

✥ *Wake Up, America!*,
a.k.a. *Armed Woman Awakening a Sleeping Man*,
a.k.a. *War*, 1941
Gouache and watercolor on paper,
4 3/16 x 5 3/8 in. / 10.7 x 13.7 cm.
Estate stamped lower right
The Stanley Collection, Portland, Maine.
This work is a study for the larger oil painting
by the same title.
SRF-MIS-39A. See SRF-MIS-39.

Winter Evening,
a.k.a. *Christmas Morning, Adirondacks*,
a.k.a. *Christmas Morning*, ca. 1945
Oil on canvas board, 11 x 15 in. / 27.9 x 38.1 cm.
Signed lower right
Private Collection.
American Artists Group greeting card No. 15 A
78, entitled, *Winter Evening*. Used for the 1946
General Electric annual calendar. Discussed on
page 569 of *It's Me O Lord* along with the painting
for the 1947 calendar depicting a New England
village common. Kent referred to the image in
the 1946 calendar as "an Adirondack valley on a
moonlit winter's night." Working from virtually
the same location, the artist created another
painting descriptively listed above as Untitled:
Christmas Evening.
SRF-MIS-40.
Works related by perspective: SRF-MIS-40a, by geography:
SRF-MIS-37.2, and by theme: SRF-MIS-2, 9, 10, 12, 13, 37.3
and 40a.

Winter Evening,
a.k.a. *Christmas Morning, Adirondacks*,
a.k.a. *Christmas Morning*, ca. 1945
Gouache and watercolor on board, 11 x 15 in. /
27.9 x 38.1 cm.
Unsigned
Private Collection.
A study for the oil by the same title (SRF-MIS-40).
Titled *Christmas Morning* and illustrated in reverse
on page 331 of *Rockwell Kent: An Anthology Of His
Work*, 1982.
SRF-MIS-40a.
Works related by perspective: SRF-MIS-40, by geography:
SRF-MIS-37.2, and by theme: SRF-MIS-9, 10, 12, 13 and 37.3.

Books by Rockwell Kent

Regarding or including material on his life in the Adirondacks.

❖ *It's Me O Lord*, 1955
Text and illustrations by Kent
New York: Dodd, Mead and Company
The manuscript for this book is in the collection of the Pushkin Museum.

❖ *This Is My Own*, 1940
Text and illustrations by Kent
New York: Duell, Sloan and Pearce
The typescript for this book is in the collection of the Pushkin Museum.

Other documents given to the Soviet Union in 1960 (now housed in the Pushkin Museum) as part of the "Great Kent Collection" gift include these manuscripts: Alaska Diary (the basis for *Wilderness*), Tierra del Fuego Diary (the basis for *Voyaging*), N by E, Salamina (first draft, and a bound copy of the final draft), and Greenland Diary; typescripts: Tierra del Fuego Diary, *Salamina,* and Greenland Diary. (For additional information see *Rockwell Kent's Forgotten Landscapes*, p. 94.)

Drawings and Prints

Compared with much of Kent's *oeuvre* in the graphic media, there are relatively few completed compositions depicting the Adirondack landscape. Many of the drawings inspired by the Adirondacks Kent created for practical purposes, such as designs for stationary and greeting cards, bookplates and marks, tourism brochures, placemats, menus, coasters, Asgaard Dairy logos, and for his own two autobiographical writings, *This Is My Own* and *It's Me O Lord*. Most of the finished drawings for these books were part of the artist's gift to the Soviet Union in 1960. Other drawings for book illustrations remain in private collections. A sample of these follows.

Drawings for Book Illustrations

Drawings for illustrations for *It's Me O Lord*, ca. 1953–54.
One life study in pencil for the title page illustration, one brush, pen and ink for the frontispiece, and 96 chapter heads in pen and ink, of which several depict Adirondack scenes.
Pushkin Museum.

Drawings for illustrations for *This Is My Own*, ca. 1939–40.
Forty-two drawings in crayon, brush and ink, and pen and ink.
Pushkin Museum.

Other drawings for illustrations for *This Is My Own* can be found in public and private collections in this country. The following are in private collections unless otherwise noted.

❖ *The Promised Land*
Pen, brush and ink, and crayon on paper,
image: 2 5/8 x 5 3/16 in. / 6.7 x 13.2 cm.
(illustration p. 19).
Rockwell Kent Gallery.

❖ *To Freedom*
Pen, brush and ink, and crayon on paper,
image: 3 5/8 x 5 1/4 in. / 9.2 x 13.3 cm.
(illustration p. 35).
Rockwell Kent Gallery.

❖ *While the Sun Shines*
Pen, brush and ink, and crayon on paper,
image: 10 x 7 in. / 25.4 x 17.8 cm.
(illustration p. 139). Adirondack Museum,
Gift of Pat Alger in memory of Jacquie and
Dan Burn Jones. 99.41.2

To Banbury Cross
Pen, brush and ink on paper,
image: 3 7/8 x 5 3/4 in. / 9.8 x 14.6 cm.
(illustration p. 67).

God Bless Our Home,
Pen, brush and ink on paper,
image: 3 7/8 x 5 3/4 in. / 9.8 x 14.6 cm.
(illustration p. 75).

Public Service
Pen, brush and ink, and crayon on paper,
image: 4 1/8 x 5 3/4 in. / 10.5 x 14.6 cm.
(illustration p. 93).

That Look
Pen, brush and ink, and crayon on paper,
image: 3 5/8 x 5 3/4 in. / 9.2 x 14.6 cm.
(illustration p. 231).

In the Name of the Great Jehovah
Pen, brush and ink on paper,
image: 4 x 5 3/4 in. / 10.2 x 14.6 cm.
(illustration p. 249).

The Nut Farm
Pen, brush and ink, and crayon on paper,
image: 4 x 5 3/4 in. / 10.2 x 14.6 cm.
(illustration p. 265).

❖ *The Vigilantes,* 1937
Pen, brush and ink, and crayon on paper,
9 1/4 x 6 1/2 in. / 23.5 x 16.5 cm.
Library of Congress, Washington, D. C.
Produced for the cover of the pamphlet *The Vigilantes Hide Behind the Flag* by Isobel Walker Soule, published by International Labor Defense, New York. A slightly altered version of this image was used as an illustration for p. 205, *This Is My Own.*

Other Adirondack-Related Drawings

✤ *Bringing Home the Christmas Tree*, ca. 1967
Pen, brush and ink on paper, 10 1/8 x 5 1/8 in. /
25.7 x 13 cm.
James and Charlene James Duguid.

Fabric designs, ca. 1950s
Opaque watercolors and/or gouache
These designs were developed into alternating
drop-repeat patterns which were printed on
heavy mercerized linen-type cloth. Of the more
than thirty designs created, several were Adirondack inspired, including *Deer Season, Harvest Time,*
and *Pine Trees.* These were printed on fabric by
Bloomcraft, Inc., of New York. "Pine boughs and
bees," "Trees and streams," and "Woodpeckers"
were never printed. Thirty designs are in the
collection of the Metropolitan Museum of Art.

✤   Samples of *Deer Season* and *Harvest Time* appeared
in the exhibit. Rockwell Kent Gallery.

Silverware and jewelry designs, ca. 1942–50
Pencil, watercolor, and/or pen
Kent created a number of designs inspired by
the Adirondack landscape that were intended
for production by Georg Jensen.

      Silverware designs include "Sheaf of Wheat,"
      "Waterfall," and "Pine Cone."

      Jewelry designs include "Sheaf of Wheat"
      and "Waterfall," and depict Asgaard Farm
      produce in "Sunflower" and "Indian Corn."
      Collections include the Rockwell Kent Gallery
      and the Metropolitan Museum of Art.

✤   Drawings for silverware and jewelry designs
      "Sheaf of Wheat," "Indian Corn," and others
      appeared in the exhibit. Rockwell Kent Gallery.

Forest Ranger, ca. 1943
Pen, brush and ink, dimensions unknown
Location unknown. Other details under research.
One of several drawings commissioned for an
advertising series for P. O. N. (Pride of Newark)
Beer, Christian Feigenspan Brewing Co., Newark,
N. J. This composition depicts the fire tower atop
and view from Palmer Hill, near Kent's home.

✤   Advertisement for P. O. N. Beer appeared
      in the exhibit. Private Collection.

✤ *The Home Decorator and Color Guide,* 1939
Sherwin-Williams Company
Written and illustrated by Kent, this catalog
includes images idealizing Gladsheim and the
Asgaard Farm property, as well as earlier homes
constructed by Kent. Previous work for Sherwin-
Williams, 1936–39, is less autobiographical.

Peace on Earth, ca. 1940–45
Pen, brush and ink on paper,
7 5/8 x 11 in. / 19.4 x 27.9 cm.
Signed lower right
Private Collection.

✤ *Scribner's Magazine* cover designs for 1928–29
Several finished compositions as well as studies
and alternates were inspired by Adirondack
scenery, including works for February (ice
harvesting), April (April showers), and December
(bringing home the Christmas tree) of 1929.

Woman in Red, ca. 1940s
Watercolor on paper, 12 x 9 in. / 30.5 x 22.9 cm.
The Rockwell Kent Legacies.

Adirondack-Related Prints

The prints with an Adirondack theme have
been catalogued by Dan Burne Jones in his book,
The Prints of Rockwell Kent: A Catalogue Raisonné, 1975.
They include (in chronological order):

✤ *Roof Tree,* 1928
Lithograph on stone. DBJ-21
Library of Congress.

Revisitation, 1928
Lithograph on zinc. DBJ-22

The Lovers, 1928
Wood engraving on maple. DBJ-23

J. C. Cowdin Dinner Invitation
and Place Card, December 1928
Lithograph on zinc and stone in four colors.
DBJ-31

Stack of Wheat, ca. 1930s
Wood engraving on maple.
DBJ-Appendix 1-U
This was printed for a variety of uses:
Asgaard Dairy products; on bags of flour;
"Asgaard / Thorough-bred / Horse Radish";
and as a postage stamp design ("Asgaard /
Postage / 4 four cents").

Mountain Climber, 1933
Wood engraving on maple. DBJ-93

Starry Night, 1933
Wood engraving. DBJ-103

✤ *Self Portrait,* 1934,
a.k.a. *Das Ding an Sich,*
a.k.a. *It's Me O Lord*
Lithograph on stone. DBJ-104
Adirondack Museum.
Gift of Pat Alger in memory of
Jacquie and Dan Burne Jones. 99.41.1

✤ *Asgaard Dairy Milk,* ca. 1935
Silk screen poster in six colors. DBJ-156
Collection Frederick Lewis.

And Women Must Weep, 1937
Lithograph on stone. DBJ-113

Good-Bye Day,
a.k.a. *The Water Carrier,* 1946
Lithograph on stone. DBJ-139

✤ *Adirondack Cabin,* 1946
Lithograph on stone. DBJ-140
Adirondack Museum. 90.11.1

✤ *Peace on Earth,* 1967
Commercial off-set lithograph
Signed lower right
Illustrated Christmas letter previously
printed as American Artists Group cards
No. 25462 and FA 29.
Private Collection.

Selected References

"$250,000." 1941. *The New Yorker* (15 November).

"A David faces the Railroad Goliath: Rockwell Kent's Battle Reverberates Outside Its Own Arena." 1930. Editorial. *Baltimore Sun*, 9 November, 13.

Ades, Dawn, et al. 1984. *The 20th-Century Poster-Design of the Avant-Garde*. Exhibition catalogue. Minneapolis, Minn.: Walker Art Center.

"Allen Yacht is Lost on Greenland Rocks." 1929. *New York Times*, 20 July, 1, 4.

"Artist Joins GE Pickets." 1946. *Schenectady Gazette*, 28 January.

Arvon, Henri. 1970. *Marxist Esthetics*. Translated by Helen Lane. Ithaca, N.Y.: Cornell University Press.

Baigell, Matthew, and Julia Williams, eds. 1986. *Artists Against War and Fascism, Papers of the First American Artists' Congress*. New Brunswick, N. J.: Rutgers University Press.

Beebe, Lucius. 1929. "Rockwell Kent, At Home." N.p., 7 April.

Buechner, Thomas S. 1972. *Norman Rockwell: A Sixty Year Retrospective*. Exhibition catalogue. New York: Bernard Danenberg Galleries.

Bullock, Florence Haxton. 1940. Review of *This Is My Own*, by Rockwell Kent. *New York Herald Tribune Books*, 24 November.

Burton, Hal. 1941. Letter, 23 October. "Ski Trails on Whiteface." *New York Herald Tribune*, n.d.

Campbell, Lawrence. 1974. "In the Matter of Rockwell Kent." *Art in America* (March/April).

Champagne, Linda. 1968. "Wandering With Champagne: Place In History," *Lake Placid News*, 3 July.

Christiansen, Carol A. 1980. "Rockwell Kent, Plattsburgh State University College and the Politics of Art." SUNY Plattsburgh Feinberg Library.

Clark, Joseph. 1950. "'What I Saw In Moscow': artist Rockwell Kent Reports on a Six-Day Visit." *Daily Worker*, 2 April.

Clark, Marcia. 1975. "A Visionary Artist Who Celebrated Wilds of America." *Smithsonian* (September).

"Dean of Painters Inspired by Bach." 1934. *Toronto Star,* 5 February.

Downs, Linda, Ellen Sharp, et. al. 1986. *Diego Rivera, A Retrospective.* Exhibition catalogue. Detroit, Mich.: Detroit Institute of Arts.

Ferris, Scott R. 1997. "Rockwell Kent Undeniably." *Chicago Art Deco Society Magazine* (Winter): 1, 24-29.

_____. 1998. "A Painter on Monhegan." *Rockwell Kent on Monhegan.* Exhibition catalogue. Monhegan Island, Maine: Monhegan Museum.

Ferris, Scott R., and Ellen Pearce. 1998. *Rockwell Kent's Forgotten Landscapes.* Camden, Maine: Down East Books.

"Funeral Services For Kent." 1971. Editorial. *Adirondack Daily Enterprise,* 15 March, 2.

Godine, Amy. 1990. "The Sally Kent Legacy." *Adirondack Life* 21 (Nov./Dec.).

Goldstein, William. 1982. Review of "The Arts and Letters of Rockwell Kent," *Publishers Weekly,* 11 June, 48-50.

Hall, Robert F. and John F. H. Gorton. 1974–1975. "Rockwell Kent's Adirondack Years." *The Conservationist* 29, (Dec./Jan.): 25-31.

Hoagland, Edward. 1996. "Drawing on a Daring Life." *Civilization* (Jan./Feb.).

Hourwich, Rebecca. 1929. "An Artist Builds a House." *Country Life* (July).

"Igloo Love." 1935. Review of *Salamina* by Rockwell Kent. *Time,* 25 November, 77.

Johnson, Fridolf, ed. 1982. *Rockwell Kent: An Anthology of His Work.* New York: Alfred A. Knopf, Inc.

Jones, Dan Burne. 1975. *The Prints of Rockwell Kent: A Catalogue Raisonné.* Chicago: University of Chicago Press.

"Kent." 1930. Editorial. *The Art Digest* 4, no. 14 (Mid-April).

"Kent, No Precedent." 1937. Editorial. *Time,* 29 November, 40.

Kent, Rockwell. 1906. Unpublished Daybook / Manuscript. Archives of American Art.

_____. 1919. "Alaska Drawings." *Arts and Decoration* (June).

_____. 1920. *Wilderness. A Journal of Quiet Adventure in Alaska.* New York: G. P. Putnam's Sons.

_____. 1924. *Voyaging Southward from the Strait of Magellan*. New York: G. P. Putnam's Sons.

_____. 1928. "Free Art in an Iron Age." *The World Tomorrow* (June): 249-250.

_____. 1930. *N by E*. New York: Brewer and Warren.

_____. 1934. Letter 11 April. "Would Preserve Whiteface, Rockwell Kent Urges That the Mountain Be Kept Inviolate." *New York Times*, n.d.

_____. 1935. *Salamina*. New York: Harcourt, Brace and Company.

_____. 1936. "'In the Name of the Great Jehovah.'" *New Masses*, 31 March, 13-14.

_____. 1937. *Rockwell Kent: Greenland Paintings and Prints*. Exhibition catalogue. Washington, D.C.: Gallery of Modern Masters.

_____. 1940. "'And That's the Story of My Life.'" *The Fraternal Outlook* 2, no. 7 (August): 10-11. Includes "Excerpts from Address by Rockwell Kent at World's Fair, June 8, 1940."

_____. 1940. *This Is My Own*. New York: Duell, Sloan and Pearce.

_____. 1941. Letter. "The Farmer's Sacrifice; They Can Hardly Do More, Rockwell Kent Argues, After Years of Struggle for Self-Preservation." *New York Herald Tribune*, 17 September.

_____. 1941. Letter, 17 October. "Ski Trails on Whiteface, Rockwell Kent Sees Defacement if Amendment Is Approved." *New York Herald Tribune*, n.d.

_____. 1942. Letter. "Rockwell Kent on Farm Prices." *New York Herald Tribune*, 1 February.

_____. 1942. *Know and Defend America: Forty Paintings of Our Country and of the Out-posts of Our Hemisphere*. New York: American Artists Group.

_____. 1944. Letter, 29 March. "Public Forum." *The Adirondack Record*, n.d.

_____. 1946. Leaflet. "The Story of The Farm of the Gods." *Cherry-Burrell Circle* (Sept./Oct.).

_____. 1948. "Goodbye" (Asgaard Dairy). *Adirondack Record Post*, 25 March. Detailed public notice of gift of Asgaard Dairy to Clifford Malkin and Floyd Plunkett, as well as ad for Whiteface Dairy, on following page.

_____. 1955. *It's Me O Lord*. New York: Dodd, Mead and Company.

_____. 1959. *Of Men and Mountains*. Ausable Forks, N.Y.: Asgaard Press.

_____. 1962. *Rockwell Kent's Greenland Journal*. New York: Ivan Obolensky, Inc.

_____. 1968. *After Long Years*. Ausable Forks, N. Y.: Asgaard Press.

Kent, Rockwell and Carl Zigrosser. 1933. *Rockwellkentiana: Few Words and Many Pictures*.
    New York: Harcourt, Brace and Company.

Kent, Sally. 1971. "Rockwell Kent's Engagement With Life." *American Dialog* (Autumn): 18-24.

Kettlewell, James K. 1974. "Rockwell Kent 1882–1971." Glens Falls: The Hyde Collection.

"Lake Placid Rally For War Fund Held By Rockwell Kent." 1941. Editorial. *New York Herald Tribune*, 29 August.

Lee, Ruth Webb. 1952. *A History of Valentines*. Wellesley Hills, Mass.: Lee Publications.

Mackinnon, Anne. 1993. "A Home to Live and Breathe. *Adirondack Life* (March/April).

_____. 1999. "I Send You All This Heart of Mine, Valentines from Rockwell Kent." *Adirondack Life* (February).

Novak, Barbara. 1980 *Nature and Culture: American Landscape Painting 1825–1875*. New York: Oxford University Press.

"Posters Used by American Industries as War Production Incentives." 1942. Boston: S. D. Warren Company (September).

Prescott, Orville. 1955. "Books of The Times." *New York Times*, 13 May.

Ridley, Mary Wells. 1941. "Rockwell Kent's Ideas on Decorating." *New York World Telegram*, 14 March.

Robert Henri and Five of his Pupils. 1946. Exhibition catalogue. New York : Century Association, 5 April to 1 June.

Robinson, Selma. 1931. "Rockwell Kent: The writer of the moment, seen by Selma Robinson." *Charm* (January).

"Rockwell Kent." 1940. Editorial. *Office and Professional News* (Nov./Dec.).

"Rockwell Kent Has Operation." 1956. *Newark Star Ledger*, 25 May.

"Rockwell Kent Home Destroyed By Fire." 1969. *Adirondack Daily Enterprise*, 18 April, 1.

"Rockwell Kent Home Destroyed By Fire Friday." 1969. *Adirondack Record-Elizabethtown Post*, 24 April, 1.

"Rockwell Kent in Hospital." 1971. *New York Times*, 5 March, 39.

"Rockwell Kent Joins Schenectady Pickets." 1946. *The Saratogian*, 28 January, 6.

"Rockwell Kents Lose Home In Fire: Artist Flees Upstate Blaze Unhurt — Aid Fund Set Up." 1969. *New York Times*, 19 April.

"Rockwell Kent Off Wednesday For Greenland." 1934. *New York Herald Tribune*, 6 July.

"Rockwell Kent and Son Depart For Greenland." 1934. N.p. 12 July.

"Rockwell Kent Sues for Passport." 1955. *Newark News*, 15 December.

Russell, Cara Green. 1941. "Rockwell Kent Writes Story of His Life. . . ." Review of *This is My Own* by Rockwell Kent. Greensboro, N. C., *Daily News*, 23 February.

Stanley. Eliot. 1989. "The Lively Poster Arts of Rockwell Kent." *Journal of Decorative and Propaganda Art* (Spring): 6-31.

Topping, Seymour. 1960. "Moscow Gets Art of Rockwell Kent." *New York Times*, 16 November.

Traxel, David. 1980. *An American Saga: The Life and Times of Rockwell Kent.* New York: Harper and Row.

Warner, John L. 1940. "Rockwell Kent at Home." *Syracuse Sunday Post-Standard* (1 December).

West, Richard V. 1985. *"An Enkindled Eye": The Paintings of Rockwell Kent.* Santa Barbara, Calif.: Santa Barbara Museum of Art.

Whitman, Alden. 1971. "Rockwell Kent, Artist, Is Dead: Championed Left-Wing Causes." *New York Times*, 14 March, 1 and 74.

Wrede, Stuart. 1988. *The Modern Poster.* Exhibition catalogue. New York: The Museum of Modern Art.

Index

"25th Annual National Art Exhibition"
exhibit, 32
"1947 / Asgaard" painted wood chest, 1

A

Aaron, Daniel, 42 *n.*6
abstract art, 4, 8
adding figures to painting, 28
Adirondack Cabin lithograph, 36–37
Adirondacks as inspiration for RK, 2, 8,
11–19
Adirondacks painting, 25, 26, 42 *n.*8
Alaska as inspiration for RK, 6, 16
American Artists Congress, 6
American Impressionism techniques, 2
American Labor Party, 15, 23
America painting, 41–42
Amiel, Henri, influence on RK, 21
Ancient Elm painting, 18, 23, 26, 27
And this, my child, is where your mother was born
painting, 42 *n.*8
And Women Must Weep lithograph, 35, 36
anti-Communist attitudes, 8
anti-Fascism cause, 40
"A Portfolio of Drawings," 35
Appelhof, Ruth Stevens, 19 *n.*4
architecture, RK interest in, 2, 24
Archives of American Art, Kent Collection
at, 19 *n.*8
Armory Show, 4
art, purpose of, 5, 8, 16–17, 40, 42
arts, graphic, 1, 6, 7, 24, 25
Asgaard Barn illustration, xv
Asgaard Dairy Milk poster, 15

Asgaard farm at Au Sable Forks, 11–13, 14–15,
16, 18, 31, 41
"Asgaard Farm" painting, vi, 3, 18, 42
Asgaard in January painting, 4, 18, 24, 28,
29, 30, 39
Asgaard's Meadows, 10, 23, 27
At Peace painting, 16, 30, 38
Au Sable Forks
farm at, 11–13, 14–15, 16, 18, 31
Rockwell Kent Legacies of, 10
village and river, 19 *n.*7
Au Sable Rapids: Adirondacks painting, 29
Au Sable River Rapids painting, 3, 18, 28

B

Bach, J. S., 21
background of RK, 1–2
Ballyhoo cartoon, 7
Bellows, George, 3
Bible, as inspiration for RK, 21
birth and childhood of RK, 1
Bowdoin College Museum of Art, 10
Bringing Home the Christmas Tree drawing, xiii
Burchfield, Charles, 27

C

Cape Cinema ceiling mural, 40
Carnegie Institute's exhibit, 32
Cassidy, Donna M., 19 *n.*5
ceiling mural at Cape Cinema, 41
Charity, 40, 43 *n.*19
Chase, William Merritt, 2, 21
Chest, Painted Wood, 1
child portraits, 27
children of RK, 11, 12, 30
Christian ethics, 23
Christmas greeting, 31

Christmas Seal art, 7, 29, 30
Christmas Tree painting, 13
civil rights, RK's interest in, 6, 37
Cloud Shadows painting, 18, 19, 23, 42
Clover Fields painting, 18, 24, 27
Cold War symbolized in RK's painting,
30, 31, 33, 34
Cole, Thomas, 23
collections of RK's letters and papers, 19 *n.*8
Columbia University and RK, 19 *n.*8, 21
commissions with Steinway and Sons, 40
communists, attitudes toward, 8
Congress, RK as candidate, 15, 23
Cortissoz, Royal, 28, 43 *n.*9
cultural diversity, 5

D

dairy farm operations, 14–15
dairy graphics, 15
dancers, RK influenced by, 29
Darwin, as inspiration for RK, 21
Davis, Stuart, 4, 14
December Eight, 1941 painting, 30, 35–36, 38
Deer on Palmer Hill painting, 25
Delaware and Hudson railroad, 13
Depression, affect on artistic style, 4, 14, 26
development of modern art, 4
diversity, cultural, 5
donation of paintings to Soviet Union, 9
Douglas, William O., 9
Dove, Arthur, 4
drawings donated to Soviet Union, 9
du Bois, Guy Pene, 3
Duncan, Isadora, 29
Duncan, Jeffrey L., 43 *n.*20

E

Edman, 22, 42 *n*.1, 2, 4, 7, 11

education of RK, 1, 3

electrotype printing techniques, 6, 25

Emerson, as inspiration for RK, 21, 22, 23, 24,
    30, 42 *n*.1, 42 *n*.6

Eternal Vigilance is the Price of Liberty lithograph, 39

ethics, Christian, 23

exhibits

    Carnegie Institute's "Painting in the
        United States," 32

    International Exhibition of Modern Art, 4

    "Know and Defend America" exhibition,
        28

    Soviet tour of RK's work, 32

    Springville "25th Annual National Art
        Exhibition," 32

F

farm at Au Sable Forks ("Asgaard"),
    11–13, 14–15, 16, 18, 31

Farnsworth Museum of Art, 43 *n*.18

Fascism, RK's attitude toward, 37, 39

Faust by Goethe, 40

Federal Art Project, 5

Figure Representing the Black Race by
    Diego Rivera, 38

figures and shapes in RK's paintings, 25, 28,
    29–33, 35, 36–38, 40, 41

Fire! lithograph, 34, 39

folk portraiture as influence on RK, 27, 29

Foreboding lithograph, 35

Forest Fires Aid the Enemy poster, 25, 34

Forest Ranger advertisement, 44

Franz, Robert, 21

From Palmer Hill painting, 32

G

galleries

    art, 8

    Richard Larcada, 9

    Rockwell Kent at SUNY Plattsburgh,
        10, 19 *n*.8

    Springville (Utah) High School, 32

Gladsheim painting, 11

Glens Falls, N.Y., The Hyde Collection, 10

God, RK's belief in, 23

Goethe's *Faust*, 40

gouache, 39

Grant, Mrs. Ernest, 7

graphic arts, 7, 24

"Great Kent Collection," 8, 43 *n*.18

Greenland

    compared to Adirondacks, 16

    as inspiration for RK, 2, 6

Green Valley painting, 32

H

Haekel, Ernst, influence on RK, 21

Hanson, Duane, 30

Harris, Carl, 43 *n*.16

Hartley, Marsden, 4

Harvest Time fabric, 1

Haskell, Barbara, 19 *n*.4

Hayt, Elizabeth, 43 *n*.10

Heavy, Heavy Hangs Over Thy Head painting,
    27, 28

Henri, Robert, 2–3, 16, 21, 23

Hitler's invasion of Soviet Union, 38

Home from School, Asgaard painting, 28

Hope Springs Eternal painting, 38, 43 *n*.18

Hopper, Edward, 3

House Committee on Un-American
    Activities, 8

human rights, RK's interest in, 6, 37

The Hyde Collection of Glens Falls, N.Y., 10

I

illustrations, book, 6, 24

Indian Corn drawing, 44

industrialization, affect on artistic style, 4

inspirations for RK

    Adirondacks, 2, 8, 11–19

    Alaska, 6, 16

    Bible, 21

    Darwin, 21

    Emerson, 21, 22, 23, 24, 30, 42 *n*.1, 42 *n*.6

    Greenland, 2, 6

    labor, 21

    life, 21, 22

    literature, 21, 22

    music, 21–22, 40

    nature, 3, 4, 16–17, 21, 28, 42

    Newfoundland, 27

    Thoreau, 21, 42, 43 *n*.20

    Tierra del Fuego, 6

    Whiteface Mountain, 16, 18

    Whitman, 21, 24

International Exhibition of Modern Art, 4

International Workers' Order, 6

Isadora Duncan and the Follies, 29

It's Me O Lord book, 7, 15, 22, 25, 35,
    43 *n*.15, 16

J

Jay, N.Y., 13, 14

Jay Taxpayers Association, 14

Jones, Dan Burne, 43 *n*.15, 43 *n*.17

K

Kazin, Alfred, 42 *n*.6

Kent, Frances (Lee), 11, 12

Kent, Kathleen, 11

Kent, Rockwell

    adding figures to painting, 28

    and Adirondack Mountains, 1, 8, 11–19

    as architectural draftsman, 2

    art, purpose of, 5, 7–8, 22, 23, 42

    birth and childhood, 1

    causes he supported, 1–2, 5, 14–15

    as chairman of Jay, [N.Y.] Taxpayers
        Association, 14

    children of, 11, 12, 30

    as Congressional candidate, 15, 23

    dairy farm operations, 14–15

    death, 10

    education, 1, 3, 21

    exhibits, 4, 9, 28, 32

    figures' shapes in paintings, 28, 29–30,
        33, 38, 40

    graphic arts, 1, 6, 7, 24, 25

    as graphic designer, 7

    as illustrator, 6

    Lenin Peace Prize, 9

    letters and papers, 19 *n.*8

    mentors, 2, 21

    method of work, 16

    as modernist, 4

    passport rescinded, 9

    philosophy of life, 6

    in Plattsburgh, 10, 19 *n.*8

    and political activities, 1–2, 6, 7, 9, 14, 15
        (*See also* socialism)

    political themes, 6, 17, 33–34

    and regionalism, 5

    and socialism, 1–2, 5–6, 8, 15, 23

    social life, 11–13

    style of, 2, 3, 4, 5, 16, 24, 26, 27, 28

    and subversive organizations, 6

    themes of (*See* themes of RK)

    war effort, support of, 14–15

Kent, Shirley / Sally (Johnstone), 10, 12,
    38, 43 *n.*13

Kent Collection at Columbia University,
    19 *n.*8

Kline, Franz, 8

"Know and Defend America" exhibition, 28

Kropotkin's *Mutual Aid a Factor of Evolution*, 21

L

labor, RK's interest in organized, 6, 15, 21, 23

Labor Party, American, 15, 23

landscape, influence on RK's works, 3, 4, 6,
    17, 42.
    See also Adirondacks; nature; wilderness

Larcada, Richard, 9, 10

Large Bather by Picasso, 38

Leaves of Grass by Walt Whitman, 25

Lehman, Herbert H., 14

Lehman, Max, 13

Lenin Peace Prize, 9

letters and papers, collections of RK's, 19 *n.*8

Lie, Jonas, 4

Life, Liberty, and the Pursuit of Happiness cartoon
    for bronze medal, 39

Life and "Art" in The New York Evening Call, 22,
    40, 43 *n.*19

life as inspiration for RK, 21, 22

light, RK's use of, 24

line cut printing techniques, 25

literature, as inspiration for RK, 21, 22

lithographs, 6, 11, 24, 34, 35, 36

Lone Woman painting, 35, 43 *n.*18

love and loss as themes, 35, 36

Loyalist cause, RK's support of, 37

luminism, 24, 42, 42 *n.*5

M

MacArthur, General, 34

Mail Service in the Tropic and Arctic Territories
    mural, 27

Maine's Bowdoin College Museum of Art, 10

Malkin, Clifford, 15

manuscripts donated to Soviet Union, 9

Marin, John, 4

Max's Restaurant, 13

McCarthy, Joseph, 8

media of RK, 1, 5, 16, 39. *See also* techniques

Melville's *Moby Dick or the Whale*, 6, 12, 25

Michaelangelo's 'Creation of Man,' 43 *n.*17

Mikhailov, Pavel P., 30–31

Miller, Kenneth Hayes, teacher of RK, 2, 21

Moby Dick or the Whale by Herman Melville,
    6, 12, 25

modern art, 4, 7

Monhegan Island, Maine, 2, 21

Mountain Climber wood engraving, 6

Mountain Road painting, 18, 24

mural at Cape Cinema, ceiling, 41

music, as inspiration for RK, 21–22, 40

Mutual Aid a Factor of Evolution, by Kropotkin, 21

My Daughter Clara painting, 27

N

National Committee for People's Rights, 6

National Tuberculosis Association, 7

nature

    influence on RK, 3, 17

    as inspiration for RK, 3, 4, 16–17,
        21, 28, 42

    as theme, 3, 4, 17, 21, 28

New Deal Art programs, 5, 8

Newfoundland as inspiration for RK, 27

New York City art movement, 8

New York School of Art, 3, 8

non-objective painting, 4

Novak, Barbara, 42 *n*.6

O

"Oh Hell! Rockwell Kent's been here!"
    Ballyhoo, 7

O'Keeffe, Georgia, 3, 4

Old Man, Old Horse, Old Barn, Old Mountains:
    Adirondacks painting, 42 *n*.8

Oncoming Storm: Adirondacks painting,
    30, 31, 32, 33, 34, 38

On Earth Peace mural, 27

On the Origin of Species, as inspiration for RK, 21

Our America series theme plate, 1

Our Seamen, Give 'Em A Hand poster, 39

P

Painted wood chest, 1

"Painting in the United States" exhibit, 32

paintings. *See also* specific titles of paintings
    abstraction or non-objective, 4
    adding figures to, 28
    donated to Soviet Union, 9
    figures and shapes in RK's, 28, 29–30,
        33, 38, 40

Palmer Hill, view from, 32

passport of RK rescinded, 9

Pastoral painting, 41

peace as theme, 6, 17, 27, 30, 38

Peace on Earth lithograph, v

Philadelphia Museum of Art, 19

Phillips, William, 34

Picasso's Large Bather, 38

Pine Tops and Mountain Peaks painting, 17, 23

plate, *Our America* series,, 1

Plattsburgh, RK in, 10, 19 *n*.8

Plunkett, Floyd, 15

poets, influence on RK, 21

political activities of RK, 1–2, 6, 7, 9.
    See also socialism

political themes of RK, 6, 17

Pollack, Jackson, 8

Porter, Fairfield, 27

portraits, child, 27

portraiture, folk, 27, 29

posters
    Forest Fires Aid the Enemy, 25, 34
    Our Seamen, Give 'Em A Hand poster, 39
    pro-democracy, 32–33
    Soviet and anti-Nazi, 43 *n*.14
    Student Christian Association Movement, 25
    "That, for their sake...", 33

Princeton University, Kent Collection at,
    19 *n*.8

printing techniques, 25

printmaking, 6

prints donated to Soviet Union, 9

pro-democracy cause, 33, 40

propaganda art, 40. *See also* posters

Public Service painting, 13

Public Works of Art Project, 5

R

Rabideau, Moses, 11

Rachmaninoff, Sergei, 40

railroad, Delaware and Hudson, 12, 13

regionalism, 4, 5, 8

Reif, Rita, 43 *n*.14

Richard Larcada Gallery, 9

Rivera, Diego, 38

Rockwell, Norman, RK compared to, 33, 40

"Rockwell Kent for Congress" broadside, 15

Rockwell Kent Gallery at SUNY Plattsburgh,
    10, 19 *n*.8

Rockwell Kent Legacies of Au Sable Forks, 10

Roof Tree lithograph, 11

Roosevelt, President Franklin D., 5, 7,
    14, 15, 34

Rosenberg, James, 2, 19 *n*.3

Rothko, Mark, 8

Russian Mass painting, 39, 40

S

Sacco, execution of, 37

Sally painting, 12

Samolhvalov, Aleksandr, 33

Schopenhauer, influence on RK, 21

Schroon Lake painting, 23

Scribner's magazines, 7

See No Evil, Hear No Evil, Speak No Evil,
    40, 43 *n*.19

Segal, George, 30

Self Portrait, opposite pg. 1

Shakespeare, 25, 40–41

Sheeler, Charles, 3

Sherwin-Williams art, 7

Skaters painting, 18, 28, 29, 30, 39

Smith, David, 8

socialism, RK's interest in, 1–2, 5–6,
    8, 15, 23, 39

social life of RK, 11–13

social realism, 3

Soffer, Miriam, 19 *n*.6

Sorrows of the World, 35

South Vietnamese Liberation Front, 9

Soviet students at Asgaard Farm, 31

Soviet Union
    donation of paintings to, 9

Hitler's invasion of, 38
tour of RK's work, 32
Spanish Civil War, RK's attitude toward, 37, 38
spokesman for mankind, 5
Spring Freshet painting, 29
Springville (Utah) High School Art Gallery
exhibit, 32
Stack of Wheat engraving, 19, 42, 80
Stallings, Lawrence, 1, 19 *n.1*
State University of New York at Plattsburgh,
10, 19 *n.8*
Steinway and Sons commissions, 40
Storm Clouds, Lake George by Georgia O'Keeffe, 3
Stravinsky's *The Fire Bird*, 40
Student Christian Association Movement poster, 25
style
and Great Depression, 4, 14, 26
of RK, 2, 3, 4, 5
subversive organizations of RK, 6
supreme expression of man's spirit, art as, 5

T

techniques. *See also* media
American Impressionism, 2
gouache, 39
printing, 25
of RK's mentors, 2
"That, for their sake..." poster, 33
Thayer, Abbott, 2, 21
The Au Sable Valley painting, 30, 32
The Complete Works of William Shakespeare, 25
The Covered Bridge at Jay painting, 18, 29
The Entrance of the Gods into Valhalla by
Wagner, 40
The Fire Bird by Stravinsky, 40
The Lovers wood engraving, 40
themes of RK

love and loss, 35, 36
nature, 3, 4, 16, 17, 18, 21, 28, 42
peace, 6, 17, 27, 30, 38
political, 6, 17, 33—34
war, 30, 31, 33, 34, 37—39,
43 *n.16*, 43 *n.17*
The Open Road painting, 35
The Vigilantes Hide Behind The Flag, 25
The Young Hammerer painting, 27
This Is My Own book, 5, 7, 16, 25
This Is My Own painting, 3, 27—28, 43 *n. 9*
Thoreau, as inspiration for RK, 21, 42, 43 *n. 20*
Tierra del Fuego, 6, 16
Tirolerland, 13
To Freedom drawing, ii
Tolstoy, Leo, 5, 22
train, Delaware and Hudson railroad, 12, 13
transcendentalists, RK's similarities to, 23
Truman, President Harry S., 34
Tuberculosis Association, 7
typography, 7

U

Un-American Activities House Committee, 8
United American Artists, 6
Untermeyer, Louis, 13
urbanization, affect on artistic style, 5

V

Vanzetti, execution of, 37
Venus and Adonis by Shakespeare, 40—41
Victorian poets, influence on RK, 21
Vietnamese Liberation Front, 9
View from Palmer Hill painting, 32

W

Wagner's *The Entrance of the Gods into*

Valhalla, 40
Wake Up, America! painting, 30, 39
Wallace, Henry, 15
war as theme, 30, 31, 33, 34, 37—39,
43 *n.16*, 43 *n.17*
war effort, RK's support of, 14—15
War painting, 37
West, Richard V., 10
"What is Art?" by Leo Tolstoy, 22
While The Sun Shines drawing, 26
Whiteface Mountain
as inspiration to RK, 16, 18
RK's opposition to road, 14
Whitman, as inspiration for RK, 21, 24
*Wilderness: A Journal of Quiet Adventure in
Alaska*, 6
wilderness as inspiration, 14, 16—17
Wilmerding, John, 43 *n.20*
Wingate, John, 43 *n.16*
"Winged Victory," 40

Winter Sunrise, Whiteface Mountain painting,
14, 24
Wood, Grant, 3
wood engraving, 24
The Lovers, 40
Mountain Climber, 6
workers in Adirondacks, temporary, 26
works donated to Soviet Union, 9
World-Famous Paintings, 20
World War II, RK's attitude toward, 37—38
writings of RK, 21

Z

Zigrosser, Carl, 6

A Note on Typography and Production

Among his formidable skills as a graphic artist, Rockwell Kent was a savvy, versatile, and talented typographer who could hand-illustrate type styles in his artwork, a skill rarely practiced today in the era of computer-generated graphics. As a designer, I appreciate having the Mac computer as a tool, and have used it exclusively in the production of this book. With it I have tried to honor Kent by incorporating type faces reflecting his interest in the Nordic and Germanic aesthetic (Charlemagne initials); his respect for the past (Caslon Open Face numerals); and his use of clean, modern sans-serif forms (Futura, designed in the 1920s, for captions). Weiss, a serif family of faces featuring the "crossed double-u" (W) Kent preferred and a compact x-height, has been employed as body and titling text, set with relatively open leading, another Kent preference.

Rockwell Kent also believed in the skill of the American worker, the talent of the local craftsman. In so keeping, this book was produced in the Adirondack Region.

JM

Stack of Wheat, ca. 1930s
Wood engraving on maple.
From "Asgaard Stone Ground
Whole Grain Flour" label.
Courtesy Ted Comstock.